Using the Internet for the Over 50s

Prentice Hall
is an imprint of

Harlow, England • London • New York • Boston • San Francisco • Toronto • Sydney • Singapore • Hong Kong
Tokyo • Seoul • Taipei • New Delhi • Cape Town • Madrid • Mexico City • Amsterdam • Munich • Paris • Milan

PEARSON EDUCATION LIMITED

Edinburgh Gate
Harlow CM20 2JE
Tel: +44 (0)1279 623623
Fax: +44 (0)1279 431059
Website: www.pearsoned.co.uk

First published in Great Britain in 2010

004.678

Pearson Education is not responsible for the content of third party internet sites.

ISBN: 978-0-273-73493-2

British Library Cataloguing-in-Publication Data
A catalogue record for this book is available from the British Library

Library of Congress Cataloging-in-Publication Data
Holden, Greg.
   Using the Internet for the Over 50s / Greg Holden.
      p. cm.
   ISBN 978-0-273-73493-2 (pbk.)
 1. Internet. 2. World Wide Web. 3. Internet and older people. I. Title.
   TK5105.875.I57H657 2010
   004.67'8–dc22
                                        2010030938

Microsoft screen shots reprinted with permission from Microsoft Corporation.
Facebook is a Trademark of Facebook Inc.

10 9 8 7 6 5 4 3 2 1
14 13 12 11 10

Typeset in 11/14 pt ITC Stone Sans by 3
Printed and bound in Great Britain by Scotprint

Using the Internet for the Over 50s

in **Simple** steps

Greg Holden

Use your computer with confidence

Get to grips with practical computing tasks with minimal time, fuss and bother.

In Simple Steps guides guarantee immediate results. They tell you everything you need to know on a specific application; from the most essential tasks to master, to every activity you'll want to accomplish, through to solving the most common problems you'll encounter.

Helpful features

To build your confidence and help you to get the most out of your computer, practical hints, tips and shortcuts feature on every page:

 ALERT: Explains and provides practical solutions to the most commonly encountered problems

 HOT TIP: Time and effort saving shortcuts

 SEE ALSO: Points you to other related tasks and information

 DID YOU KNOW? Additional features to explore

WHAT DOES THIS MEAN?

Jargon and technical terms explained in plain English

Practical. Simple. Fast.

Dedication:

To my father.

Author's acknowledgements:

Once again, I want to acknowledge the help and support provided by Ann Lindner.

Publisher's acknowledgements:

We are grateful to the following for permission to reproduce copyright material:

Photos: Linksys website http://www.linksys.com, pp.4, 39, 51, 205.

Screenshots: Google website: http://www.google.co.uk, pp.7, 8, 83, 86, 87, 118; Facebook website: www.facebook.com, pp.16, 31, 165, 166, 167, 168, 169, 170, 171, 172, 173, 174; Fast.co.uk.: www.fast.co.uk Broadband ISP, p.26; Mozilla Thunderbird website: http://www.mozilla.com, p.29; Virgin Media website: http://www.virginmedia.com, p.35; Linksys website: http://www.linksys.com, pp.42 and 43; Symantec website: http://www.Symantec.com, pp. 94 and 101; Experian Limited website http://www.experian.co.uk, p.108; Harrods website: http://www.harrods.com/harrodsstore/, pp.10, 11, 113; http://www.harrods.com/HarrodsStore/find/c/ accessories,accforhim,accforhimties, p. 113, http://www.harrods.com/HarrodsStore/ShoppingBag, p.113; English Country Cottages website: http://www.english-country-cottages.co.uk, p.115. Copyright The Hoseasons Group Limited. Used with permission of the Hoseasons Group Ltd; UK Genealogy Archives website: http://uk-genealogy.org.uk, p.116; Financial Times website http://www.ft.com/home/uk, p.117; Bristol-Link website: http://www.bristol-link.co.uk, p.118; The Camping and Caravanning Club website: http://www.thefriendlyclub.co.uk, p.124; Spanglefish website: http://www.spanglefish.com, p.125; Amazon website: http://www.amazon.co.uk. © Amazon.com Inc. and its affiliates. All rights reserved, pp.129, 196-8; Skype website: http://www.skype.com, pp.175, 176, 178, 179; Tesco Direct website: http://direct.tesco.com/q/ R,100-6294.aspx, p.177; OTRNow website: http://www.otrnow.com, Used by permission of Star Creations Inc and OTRNow.com, pp.12, 13, 131; CafePress website: http://www.cafepress.com/cp/ info/sell/, p.199, http://www.cafepress.com/join.aspx, p.199, http://www.cafepress.com/products/ addProducts.aspx, p.200, http://www.cafepress.com, p.200; Microsoft screen shots reprinted with permission from Microsoft Corporation.

In some instances we have been unable to trace the owners of copyright material, and we would appreciate any information that would enable us to do so.

Contents at a glance

Contents

3 Starting to use a Web browser

7 Enjoying entertainment on the internet

8 Sending and receiving email

Top 10 Internet Problems Solved

Top 10 Tips to Get You Started

Tip 1: Make sure your computer is internet ready

In order to get on the internet, your computer has to have a network card installed. Almost all new computers sold today have one built in. But if you aren't sure what you have in your computer, you can check it yourself.

1. Check in the system tray – the set of mini program icons that appears next to your clock in the corner of your desktop.

2. Click the network connection icon in the system tray. If you see a message that says Wireless Network Connection, that indicates your computer is equipped with a wireless card already.

3. You can also check in a more systematic way. Begin by clicking the Start button in the corner of your desktop.

4. When the Start menu appears, choose Computer.

DID YOU KNOW?

Some applications store icons in the system tray so you can access them quickly. Right-click an icon and you can perform operations in the program.

5 When Windows Explorer opens, click System properties.

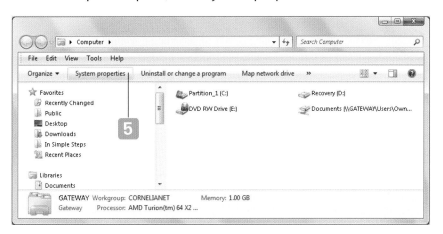

6 When the System information screen appears, click Device Manager.

7 Click the arrow next to Network adapters.

8 Scan the list of adapters installed in your computer. If you see one that says Ethernet, that means you have an Ethernet adapter and can connect to the internet with an Ethernet cable. If you see Wireless, it means you can connect to the internet wirelessly.

Control Panel Home

Device Manager —— **6**
Remote settings
System protection
Advanced system settings

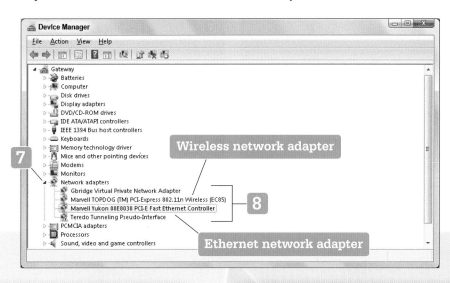

ALERT: You also need a wireless router to establish a wireless connection to the internet. See Chapter 2 for more information.

DID YOU KNOW?
You can use hardware devices to check the status of other hardware you use, such as microphones, speakers, a mouse, and so on.

Tip 2: Connect to the internet at home

The internet is worldwide and there are many connections, but how do you get that connection to your home computer? Once you sign up with an internet service provider and commit to paying a monthly or yearly access fee, if necessary, the provider runs a high-speed access line to your home. The line goes to a piece of hardware called a modem. You then connect that modem to your computer with a special high-speed networking cable that uses the Ethernet communications protocol.

1 Connect physically to a wired network by plugging your Ethernet cable into the Ethernet port on your computer. This port looks like a phone jack but it is slightly wider. Your ISP should provide you with a length of cable and a modem. (You may have to rent the modem for a small monthly fee.)

2 Plug the other end of the cable into your cable or DSL modem and make sure it is plugged in. A light will usually indicate that the modem is switched on.

? DID YOU KNOW?

If your computer does not automatically connect to the network, you may need to enable network discovery. See the Top 10 internet Problems Solved section at the end of this book.

3 A Set Network Location window will appear after your computer automatically connects. Your screen may have such options as Home, Work or Public location. Select Home network.

4 Click Close.

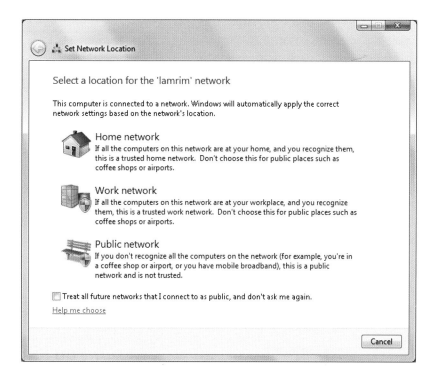

Tip 3: Navigate to a website

Your first order of business is to type in a URL (uniform resource locator) and go to a website. URLs and website names (as far as we're concerned just now) start with http:// www. I don't want to go into detail about why this is, but suffice it to say, in almost all instances you'll need to type this first. After the www., you'll type the website's name. Often this is the name of the company, such as Amazon or Microsoft, and its ending, which is often .com, .edu, .gov, .org, or .net.

1 Click once in the Internet Explorer address box. Any text that is already in the box will be highlighted so that you can type over it.

2 Type the URL of a website you want to visit and press Enter.

HOT TIP: Just because your software may come with a web browser doesn't mean you have to use the same one all the time. I'm partial to Firefox. To download and install it, go to www.mozilla.org.

 DID YOU KNOW?

.com is the most popular website ending – it means the website is a company, business, or personal site. .edu is used for educational institutions, .gov for government entities, .org for non-profit organisations (mostly), and .net for miscellaneous businesses and companies, or personal websites. There are others, though, including .info, .biz, .tv, and .uk.com.

DID YOU KNOW?

When a website name starts with https://, it means it's secure. When purchasing items online, make sure the payment pages have this prefix.

WHAT DOES THIS MEAN?

Home page: The webpage that opens when you open Internet Explorer 8 (IE8). You can set the home page and configure additional pages to open as well.

Load: A webpage must 'load' before you can access it. Some pages load instantly, while others take a few seconds.

Navigate: The process of moving from one webpage to another or viewing items on a single webpage. Often the term is used as follows: 'click the link to navigate to the new webpage.'

Website: A group of webpages that contain related information. Microsoft's website has information about Microsoft products, for instance.

URL: The information you type to access a website, such as http://www.microsoft.com.

Tip 4: Explore how search engines work

There's an old saying that it's not what you know, it's how you use it. On the Web, it's not what is out there but how to find it. A search engine is nothing more than a really big database. A program called a spider visits lots of webpages and indexes their contents. When you search for a word or phrase, the search engine scans that database to find results. Here's what to do your first time out.

1. Start up Internet Explorer and go to the most popular search engine. It's called Google, and its URL is www.google.co.uk.

2. Type a keyword or other term into the search box.

3. Specify where you want Google to search: click the web to search the entire World Wide Web, or pages from the UK.

4. Click Google Search or press Enter.

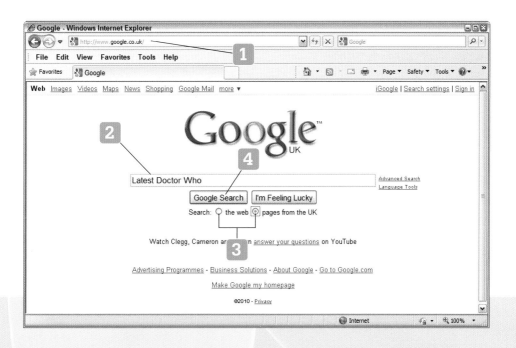

5 When your options appear, click on the most likely one to browse for a particular type of Web content.

Although Google is the most popular search engine, you have other choices. Some are listed below:

Site	URL
Google	www.google.co.uk
Bing!	www.bing.com
Yahoo!	uk.yahoo.com
Live Search	www.live.com
Ask	uk.ask.com
My Web Search	www.mywebsearch.com

Tip 5: Set your browser's security level

It seems there's always a trade-off. If you like your web sessions to be super interesting and interactive, you have your pick of a vast array of webpages with small programs, scripts, and other forms of active content. But you will have to pay a big price for your pleasure if this program, which is your primary interface to the internet, turns out to be a portal for bad things that can harm your files. When you set your security level high, you can run only less active content. The choice is yours.

1 Start up IE8.

2 Click Tools.

3 Click internet Options.

4 Click the Security tab.

5 Click internet.

6 Click and drag the Security level for this zone slider to the level you want.

7 Click OK.

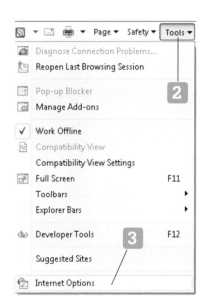

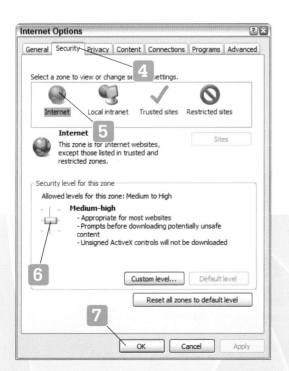

? DID YOU KNOW?

If you trust a website, you can use the Medium security level for it. Instead of clicking internet, click Trusted sites, click Sites, type the address, and click Add.

Tip 6: Make an online purchase

Going to a bricks-and-mortar store is not always necessary any more. Think about it. On days when the weather is bad or you're not able to get out, you can comparison shop all you like from the comfort of your home. You have an endless array of merchandise and services. Your purchase is promptly delivered right to your doorstep. What's not to love?

1 Find a site you like and register, if prompted to do so. You'll find a list of online stores in the UK at http://www.topoftheshops.co.uk.

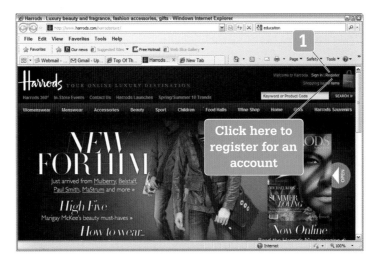

2 Browse all you like until you've picked out the goods you wish to purchase.

3 Place your selections in a shopping basket by clicking a button next to the item labelled 'Add to Cart' or 'Add to Basket', for instance.

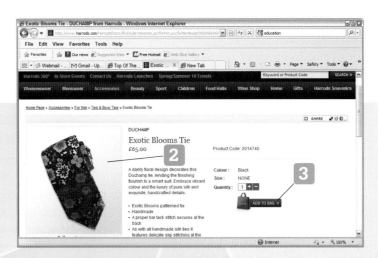

4 Review what you have in your basket, delete any items you don't want, and proceed to the checkout.

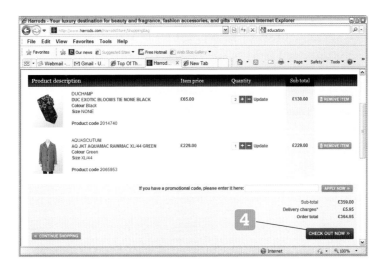

5 Enter your shipping information and make your payment.

ALERT: Don't respond to an email offer unless you've asked the company to send you information. Look for an 'https' instead of an 'http' in the URL. This indicates that the site is secure.

HOT TIP: You can even shop for groceries online. Supermarkets such as Tesco, Safeway, and Sainsbury have websites where you can make purchases and have food delivered to you. You'll find a list of online supermarkets at http://www.somucheasier.co.uk/ supermarkets-uk.html.

Tip 7: Tune into internet radio

Yes, I listen to radio all day and all night. And I'm very particular about my programming. I like specific kinds of music, much of which is offbeat and can't be found on my local commercial (AM or FM) radio stations. A whole world of music, comedy and discussion awaits you when you tune into online radio. You can use Windows Media Player as your radio 'tuner', or find a website that has an internet radio stream and use a built-in player.

1 One way to find internet radio is to search for a topic on Google – for instance, 'Old Time Radio' – and go to a website that offers a radio stream.

2 Click on a link labelled Listen Live, Webcasts, or Live Stream, or something similar.

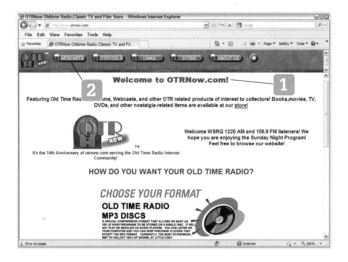

3 Many sites, like the one shown here, give you a choice of players. They provide their own – a player that pops up in a new browser window – or let you use your own software. Click the Listen with Our Player option for the pop-up window.

? DID YOU KNOW?

'Streaming' is the process of continually posting an audio file to a web server so that others can listen to it online. The effect is the same as a conventional AM or FM radio station – except that you can listen to sites from anywhere on the internet rather than just in your local area.

4 When the pop-up player opens, the audio will start playing automatically. Click Mute to silence the audio.

5 Click the Volume control to turn the sound up or down.

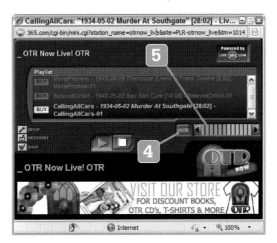

6 To use Windows Media Player as a radio 'tuner', click Start and choose Windows Media Player (or click the Windows Media Player icon near the Start button) to start up the application.

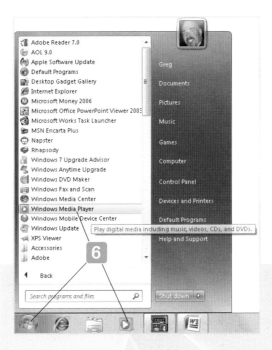

7 Click Guide.

8 Click internet Radio.

9 Choose the genre you want to listen to.

10 Click a radio station from the list displayed. The station starts playing.

HOT TIP: In addition to the process described above, many over-the-air radio stations stream live broadcasts from their home pages. Look for the website of the radio station in your home town, or anywhere around the world. Many will have a Webcast or Listen Live link that lets you listen to them instantly.

Tip 8: Compose and send a message

Much of the time, rather than responding to someone else's message, you'll be composing one from scratch. The process is almost the same as for responding to a message. But you need to make sure you have the correct email address for your recipient(s).

 HOT TIP: Be precise when writing your subject line so your recipients can easily recall what the email was about.

1 Click Create Mail.

 Create Mail

2 In the To field, type the email address for the recipient.

3 Type a subject in the Subject field.

4 Type the message in the body pane.

5 Click Send.

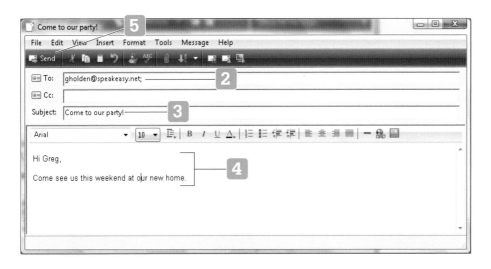

 HOT TIP: If you are sending your email to more than one recipient, separate each email address with a semicolon. The easy way to do this is to choose Tools and then click Select recipients to quickly add recipients from your Contacts list.

? DID YOU KNOW?
If you want to let someone know what's in the email but don't expect them to respond, you can put them in the Cc line. If you don't want others to know that you sent the email to someone else, you can put them in the Bcc line.

Tip 9: Comment on someone's Facebook posting

Conversations on Facebook happen in a couple of ways. You can click on the Chat box in the bottom right-hand corner of a Facebook page and chat with someone who is online. Or you can comment on someone else's post – or someone's comment to someone's post. The resulting series of remarks forms a discussion.

1 To post a reply in response to someone else's posting, click once in the Write a comment link underneath it.

2 When a text box appears, type your comment.

3 Click Comment.

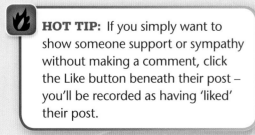

HOT TIP: If you simply want to show someone support or sympathy without making a comment, click the Like button beneath their post – you'll be recorded as having 'liked' their post.

Tip 10: Set up an eBay store

Who would have guessed that you'd end up as a shopkeeper? eBay gives everyone the chance to set up a virtual storefront for a modest monthly fee. Still, even if your items sell only once in a while, it's a good option to get rid of some of that clutter and pad your pockets in the process.

1 Go to eBay's UK site (http://www.ebay.co.uk).

2 Click Sign in, and sign in with your eBay username and password.

3 Go to the eBay Shops hub page (http://stores.shop.ebay.co.uk/_stores/hub).

4 Click Open a Shop.

? DID YOU KNOW?

A Basic Shop costs £13.03 per month, a Featured Shop costs £43.47 per month, and an Anchor Shop costs £304.34 per month.

5 Click the button next to Basic Shop.

6 Type a name for your shop.

7 Click Continue.

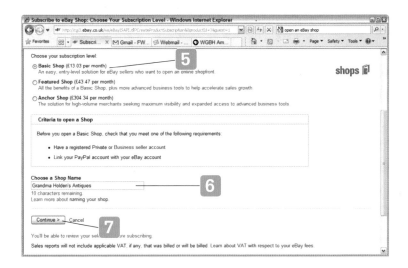

8 On the next two pages, select features, review terms and the monthly fee, and click Subscribe.

9 Once you have opened your shop, you can create sales categories for it, and add items for sale.

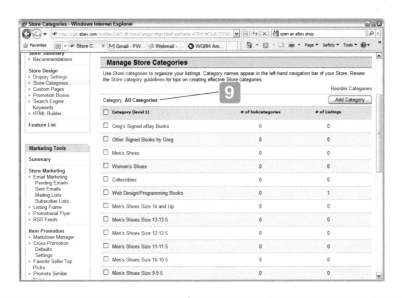

? DID YOU KNOW?
In order to open an eBay shop, you need to have a registered private or business seller account, or link your eBay account and an account with the electronic payment service PayPal (https://www.paypal.com).

HOT TIP: If you run out of space after typing 250 characters in the description, you can fill in the store specialities box to add more detail.

1 Getting started

Introduction

Everywhere you go, people seem to be talking about the internet. You hear about it on the news; your children and grandchildren periodically ask if you have 'gone online' or if you are 'on Facebook'. Have you ever wondered what it all means? Does it seem too complicated and technical for you even to get started? Take heart: the internet is well within your reach. You can join the countless individuals over the age of 50 (and 60, and 70, and even the 83-year-old Jewish grandmother who has become the star of a US cooking show called 'Feed Me Bubbe') who have embraced the chance to make new friends and keep in touch with family by going online.

This chapter leads you up the learning curve in gentle steps. You learn how the internet works by exploring some basic concepts.

What is the internet?

You've no doubt heard of the internet, but do you really understand what it is? The internet can be likened to the telephone system: it's a method of communication that links people together. There are many telephone systems in your area and around the world, and they all connect to each other so that people can get in touch and share information. Some talk over telephone wires, some use wireless phones. The internet, too, is an interconnected set of networks that joins computers, either with cables or wirelessly.

1 The internet began as a US Department of Defense project in the 1960s, sponsored by the Advance Research Projects Agency (DARPA). Once you learn how to use a web browser, you can read about its history by typing www.darpa.mil/history.html in its address box and pressing Enter.

2 It's a worldwide network of networks. Some sections of the internet serve as an especially high-speed part called the backbone. One of the backbone networks in the UK is shown here.

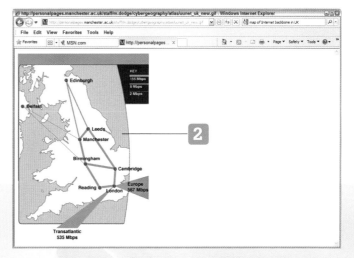

3 You 'plug in' to the internet using your computer. You connect to the internet either with a cable or wirelessly, depending on your computer's capabilities. You gain access to the internet from an internet service provider (ISP), which provides a connection to your home.

 DID YOU KNOW?

The name 'internet' came into use in the 1970s, when the internet began to expand from defence and research institutes to include universities, government departments and some businesses.

 DID YOU KNOW?

The internet uses a variety of cables and connection methods to connect computers around the globe. Some people use telephone lines, while others use fibre optic cables. But wireless connections are becoming more and more common.

What is the World Wide Web?

The internet is the big worldwide network of computers. But when people talk about the internet, they talk about things like 'websites,' 'web surfing', and so on. They are referring to the World Wide Web, a set of information within the internet that is especially user friendly. Information on the Web can include images, colours, sounds, video, and hyperlinks that take you from one location to another with a single mouse click. The World Wide Web was invented in 1990 by Tim Berners-Lee and Robert Cailliau.

1. The World Wide Web (or Web, or WWW for short) is a part of the internet that lets computer users view text, images, colours, and navigate by hyperlinks. Every webpage has an address called a URL that begins with http://.

2. Click on hyperlinks to jump to other pages or view images, video, or other content.

3. You view webpages with software called a web browser. The browser Internet Explorer (IE) comes built in with Windows. (Version 8 of Internet Explorer comes with Windows 7.) IE offers multiple tabs, each of which displays a single webpage.

4. The left or back button takes you to the previous page; the right or forward button returns you to the page you were on before you went back.

Understand how the internet works

You don't have to understand every technical detail about the internet in order to start using it. But an overview of how information gets from remote services to your computer at home will help you understand why some content is simple, some takes longer to appear, and some things like multimedia files require add-on software.

1 The internet is a *server–client* system. Computers with information called *servers* connect to the internet and are available round the clock. They make information available.

2 Your computer functions as the client. You locate a server by its address, which is called a uniform resource locator (URL).

3 To get information from a server on the internet requires software. In most cases, a web browser such as Internet Explorer will enable you to view what you need. In some cases – for instance, with audio files – you'll need a program such as Windows Media Player.

WHAT DOES THIS MEAN?

Server: A computer that is equipped with special server software and that makes files available to other computers on a network.

Client: A computer on a network that can connect to a server and access information stored on it.

Network: A group of two or more computers that can find one another and share information.

Hyperlink: A word, phrase, image, or other object that is linked to a file, image or other object. Click on the link, and your web browser jumps to the linked object.

Status bar: The small horizontal bar at the bottom of a web browser.

4 Once you have a connection, the right software, and know the address of the server, you put all these pieces together and request information from the server. You either type your address in your browser's address bar and press Enter, or click on a link that connects you to a file on a server.

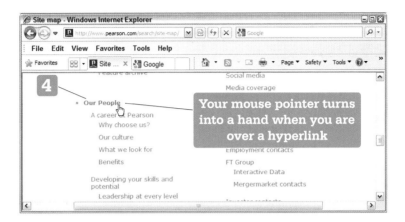

5 When data is being transferred from the server to your computer, you'll see a message in your browser's status bar notifying you of the progress.

Make sure you have what you need to get online

In order to get connected to the internet, you need to have the right computer equipment. Specifically, you need a computer that has enough speed and memory to browse websites. You also need a computer that is capable of connecting to a network such as the internet.

1 You need to get a connection from an ISP. An ISP is a phone or cable company that gives customers access to the internet, often for a fee.

2 You need a computer with a network card.

3 You need a browser and an email account.

? DID YOU KNOW?

You can also get on the internet at your local library, which probably has one or more computers available to patrons for public access.

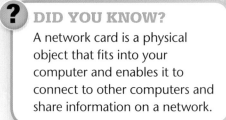

? DID YOU KNOW?

A network card is a physical object that fits into your computer and enables it to connect to other computers and share information on a network.

Make sure your computer is internet ready

In order to get on the internet, your computer has to have a network card installed. Almost all new computers sold today have one built in. But if you aren't sure what you have in your computer, you can check it yourself.

1 Check in the system tray – the set of mini program icons that appears next to your clock in the corner of your desktop.

2 Click the network connection icon in the system tray. If you see a message that says Wireless Network Connection, that indicates your computer is already equipped with a wireless card.

3 You can also check in a more systematic way. Begin by clicking the Start button in the corner of your desktop.

4 When the Start menu appears, choose Computer.

? DID YOU KNOW?

Some applications store icons in the system tray so you can access them quickly. Right-click an icon and you can perform operations in the program.

5 When Windows Explorer opens, click System properties.

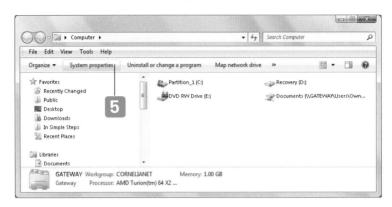

6 When the System information screen appears, click Device Manager.

7 Click the arrow next to Network adapters.

8 Scan the list of adapters installed in your computer. If you see one that says Ethernet, that means you have an Ethernet adapter and can connect to the internet with an Ethernet cable. If you see Wireless, it means you can connect to the internet wirelessly.

Control Panel Home

Device Manager

Remote settings

System protection

Advanced system settings

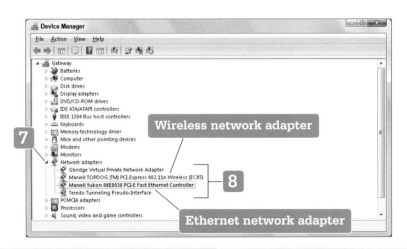

Wireless network adapter

Ethernet network adapter

ALERT: You also need a wireless router to establish a wireless connection to the internet. See Chapter 2 for more information.

? DID YOU KNOW?
You can use hardware devices to check the status of other hardware you use, such as microphones, speakers, a mouse, and so on.

Familiarise yourself with internet services

What can you do on the internet? You can take advantage of common services. The Web and email are probably the best known. Each one lets you view information or communicate with others in a particular way.

1 The World Wide Web presents information in the form of webpages. A group of pages that is linked together and is created by the same person or company is called a website. (Here, you see a list of pages that make up the Pearson Education website.) Countless webpages are being created all the time on any number of topics.

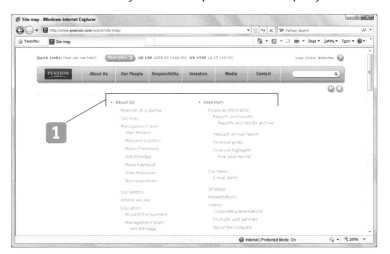

2 Electronic mail, or email, allows you to exchange typed messages with others. Once you send a message on the internet it arrives in seconds, in contrast to traditional postal mail.

3 You can type messages to others in real time and hold virtual conversations called chat sessions by using a service called either 'chat' or instant messaging (IM for short).

4 You can watch videos on YouTube or listen to internet radio as well.

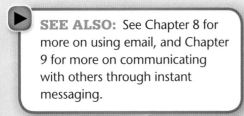

SEE ALSO: See Chapter 8 for more on using email, and Chapter 9 for more on communicating with others through instant messaging.

What can you do on the internet?

You can read about the many wonderful features of the internet in a book, but you don't really appreciate its value until you discover it for yourself. My 81-year-old father didn't really understand what he could do on the internet until he took some classes and began to explore it himself. Here are just a few examples of the things you can do online.

1 Look up information. You can check the weather quickly online without having to wait for a radio or television broadcast.

2 Keep in touch with friends and family. You may see some relatives only a few times a year. But sites such as Facebook let you know what people are up to much more frequently.

3 Buy and sell. Do you need to clean out your wardrobe? Are you looking for a bargain? Turn to sites such as eBay to do your shopping with your fingertips without having to drive to the shops.

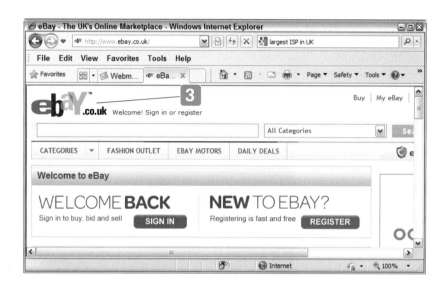

2 Getting connected to the internet

Introduction

You've probably heard the internet described as an 'information superhighway'. You may also have asked yourself: 'Where is the smoothest access to that highway?' One of the biggest and most important decisions you have to face, when you're thinking about going online, is what kind of connection is best for you and what internet service provider.

In order to get on the internet, you need to sign an agreement with a company that is in the business of providing such connections – an ISP. This process can be complex and confusing, mostly because cable companies, phone companies, and other organisations that provide internet connections offer a dizzying array of options and don't always explain them clearly. On top of that, new services are coming up all the time. It's hard to know which choice is best for you. This chapter will explain the options and lead you through the process of selecting the provider that's best for your needs.

Choose an internet service provider

I'm sure you've seen signs in hotel lobbies and coffee shops announcing that they are 'Wi-Fi hotspots'. If you have a laptop computer, a wireless card is included that lets you make a wireless connection when you're on the road. It no doubt also has a wireless port that allows you to make a wired connection from a hotel or a library. But most of the time you'll be at home. That's when you'll need an ISP for your connection. That's a company that exists to get you online, usually for a monthly fee. Most providers also offer an email service, the ability to browse the internet and space to store files and create webpages.

1 Nowadays most cable television services also offer internet access. If you already subscribe, see how much more it would cost a month to make them your ISP.

2 Also check with the company that provides your telephone service. Many of them offer internet access as well – or vice versa.

3 It always pays to comparison shop. Sites such as Broadband-Finder (www.broadband-finder.co.uk) or Broadband Checker (www.broadbandchecker.co.uk) allow you to compare prices and services all on one site.

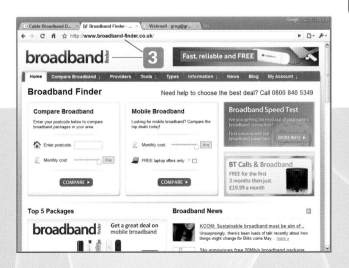

HOT TIP: If you can get a cable or phone provider to offer multiple services, it's likely to cost you less than if you paid for them separately. I'd start out with the provider of your mobile phone service, your cable service or your existing satellite service. If you order a package of phone, TV, and internet services you'll probably find you have saved some money after you crunch the numbers.

Select a type of internet connection

Cable television and telephone providers are popular as ISPs because their connections are much faster than the third option, a dial-up connection. Wireless, broadband and dial-up are all means to get to the same end: having internet access. Which is best for you depends on how much you'll use the internet, how fast and reliable you want your service to be, and how much you want to pay.

1 A dial-up connection is by far the slowest option. You use a conventional phone line to connect to a server; your computer literally dials a phone number. Your ISP will give you a list of local access numbers. Be sure to call the one that's closest to you so your phone provider doesn't charge you for long-distance calls.

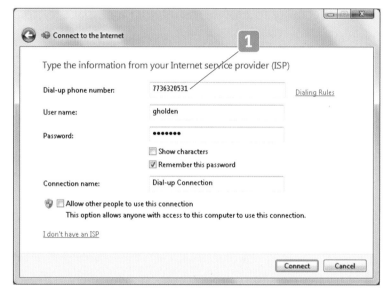

2 A digital subscriber line (DSL) connection uses the conventional copper phone lines that come into your house. DSL gives you a 'broadband' connection, which is high speed compared with dial-up connections.

3 Cable TV providers give you the fastest type of connection for home use. Cable connections also require a monthly fee, but in this case you pay the cable company rather than the phone company.

4 Wireless hotspots are connections provided by cafés, airports, hotels and other public spaces. If your laptop computer has a wireless network card and you are within range of a hotspot, you can connect automatically and get on the internet.

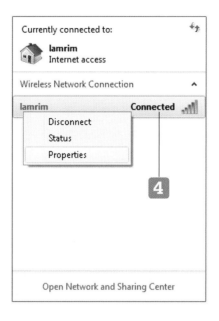

Table 2.1 internet connection types

Connection	Typical speed
Dial-up	56 Kbps (kilobits per second)
DSL	684 Kbps (684,000 bits per second)
Cable	1–3 Mbps (megabits per second)

? DID YOU KNOW?

DSL and cable connections aren't available in every area, though they are becoming more widespread. Check with your local internet providers to catalogue your choices and costs.

Connect to the internet at home

The internet is worldwide and there are many connections, but how do you get that connection to your home computer? Once you sign up with an internet service provider and commit to paying a monthly or yearly access fee, if necessary, the provider runs a high-speed access line to your home. The line goes to a piece of hardware called a modem. You then connect that modem to your computer with a special high-speed networking cable that uses the Ethernet communications protocol.

1 Connect physically to a wired network by plugging your Ethernet cable into the Ethernet port on your computer. This port looks like a phone jack but is slightly wider. Your ISP should provide you with a length of cable and a modem. (You may have to rent the modem for a small monthly fee.)

2 Plug the other end of the cable into your cable or DSL modem and make sure it is plugged in. A light will usually indicate that the modem is switched on.

3 A Set Network Location window will appear after your computer automatically connects. Your screen may have such options as Home, Work or Public location. Select Home network.

4 Click Close.

DID YOU KNOW?

If your computer does not automatically connect to the network, you may need to enable network discovery. See the Top 10 internet Problems Solved section at the end of this book.

Set Network Location

Select a location for the 'lamrim' network

This computer is connected to a network. Windows will automatically apply the correct network settings based on the network's location.

3

Home network
If all the computers on this network are at your home, and you recognize them, this is a trusted home network. Don't choose this for public places such as coffee shops or airports.

Work network
If all the computers on this network are at your workplace, and you recognize them, this is a trusted work network. Don't choose this for public places such as coffee shops or airports.

Public network
If you don't recognize all the computers on the network (for example, you're in a coffee shop or airport, or you have mobile broadband), this is a public network and is not trusted.

☐ Treat all future networks that I connect to as public, and don't ask me again.

Help me choose

Cancel

SEE ALSO: If you want to get more than one computer online, you'll need another piece of hardware called a router. See the next task for how to use one.

Connect a router

You may have only one computer in your home, but if you have more than one, you need a router. A router is what allows a broadband internet connection to be shared with other computers on your network. You also need a wireless router if you want to connect to the internet from anywhere in your home without having to plug an Ethernet cable into your computer (provided your computer is equipped with a wireless card).

1 Unplug your DSL or cable modem.

2 Take your router out of the packaging and position it in a spot close to the DSL or cable modem so they can connect easily.

3 Connect the router and modem together with a length of Ethernet cable. (You will have to unplug the cable from your computer if it was connected previously to the modem. Now you will connect it to the router.) Plug the cable into the port on the router labelled 'internet'.

? **DID YOU KNOW?**

All routers are equipped with 3–5 Ethernet ports. That means you can connect up to five computers or other devices (such as printers) in a home network. Even wireless routers include Ethernet ports. This enables you to use wireless and wired connections in the same household. You might want to use Ethernet for some computers if wireless signal strength is weak to part of your home.

HOT TIP: If you are using a wireless router, you'll get better signal quality to your laptops or wireless-enabled desktop computers by positioning the router in a central location in your residence. That way the wireless signal will reach all parts of your home with equal strength.

Position your wireless router

If you decide to go wireless, you'll need a wireless router. Give some thought to where you place your router because that location might affect the quality of your wireless signal, particularly if you have environmental factors that could cause interference. Sketch out the number of computers in your house and the devices you want to connect to your network, including the modem that connects you to the internet. Then find a central location where your wireless router will reach them all with adequate signal strength.

1 Avoid positioning the router too far away from the computers that need to use them.

2 A more central location will reach your computer and any other devices (such as printers) you may want to network.

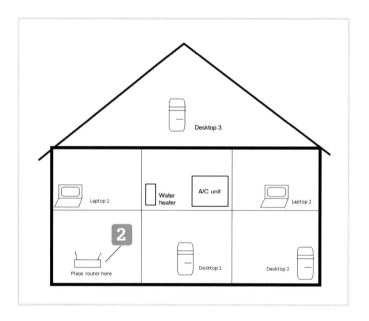

HOT TIP: Try making a mobile phone call or getting a signal on your mobile from different locations in your home. This isn't a scientific test by any means, but if you experience trouble getting a signal in certain locations, it's an indication that you may have wireless computer connection problems in those same locations.

ALERT: Plumbing, brick walls and even devices that emit radio signals can interrupt your signal. Try to avoid distances of 15–30 metres or more, or obstacles in the signal path such as major appliances or heating/cooling equipment.

Configure your wireless router, part 1

Once you physically connect your router to your DSL or cable modem and also to your computer, the next step is to configure the router so that it connects to your ISP's servers. Your ISP may provide you with software to configure your router automatically. If not, you can easily do it yourself. Just be sure to get the IP addresses of your ISP's DNS servers beforehand.

1 Click Start.

2 Choose Internet Explorer to start up your web browser.

3 Type the default IP address for your router, such as 192.168.1.1, in Internet Explorer's address box. The exact IP address depends on the brand of router you have. Table 2.2 lists IP addresses for some of the more popular router brands.

Internet Explorer

Table 2.2 Default router addresses and logins

Router manufacturer	IP address	User name	Password
Belkin	192.168.2.1	(No field provided)	(Leave blank)
D-Link	192.168.0.1	admin (lowercase)	(Leave blank)
Linksys	192.168.1.1	(Leave blank)	admin (lowercase)
Netgear	192.168.0.1	admin (lowercase)	password (lowercase)

WHAT DOES THIS MEAN?

IP: Stands for internet protocol. IP provides a standard addressing system so computers can find each other on a network such as the internet. Most addresses in the version of IP that is most widely used take the form of four numbers separated by dots, such as 192.168.34.2.

DNS (domain name service) servers: The servers to which your router connects. They allow you to connect to websites by typing user-friendly domain names such as www.google.co.uk into your browser's address bar.

4 When you're prompted for a user name and password, enter the default credentials listed in Table 2.2, and then click OK.

5 Enter the server address information given to you by your ISP when you signed up for its service. If you don't have the information, ask for it by calling your ISP's technical support staff. You'll need the IP address of your ISP's gateway, the subnet mask, and the IP address(es) of the ISP's DNS server(s).

6 Click the Save Settings button at the bottom of the tab.

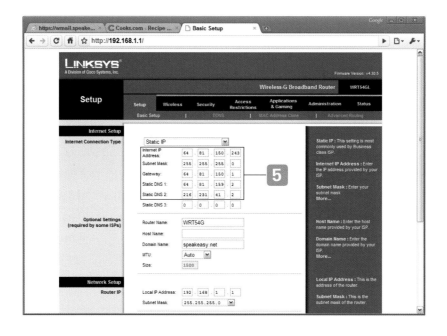

Configure your wireless router, part 2

Once you have connected to your router and entered the server addresses as described in the preceding task, you should name your network and assign a password.

Otherwise, people driving by (known as 'wardrivers') and your neighbours will be able to go online using your connection.

1 Connect to your router, if necessary, by following steps 1–3 in the preceding task.

2 When your router's configuration screen appears, click Wireless.

3 Type a name for your wireless network in the Wireless Network Name (SSID) box.

4 Click Wireless Security.

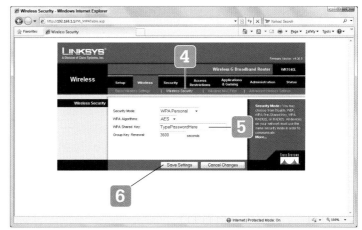

5 Type a password that you will use to access the internet through your wireless connection.

6 Click Save Settings.

 DID YOU KNOW?

It's a good idea to change your router user name and password as soon as possible. That prevents another person from being able to connect to your router.

 **HOT TIP:** A good password has at least eight characters, a mixture of numerals and alphanumeric characters, and uppercase and lowercase letters. If you must write down your security key, be sure to keep it in a safe place. Wireless Equivalent Privacy (WEP) has additional requirements: it must be either exactly 5 or 13 characters or 10 or 26 characters using 0–9 or A–F.

Run your cable through walls

If you don't have a wireless router, you need to run Ethernet cable between your modem or router and your computer. Your goal is to string cable in such a way that it causes the least damage and is as unobtrusive as possible. If you can drill a single hole between adjacent walls, that's a good set-up. Otherwise, run the cable next to the skirting board (the wooden trim just above your floor) and fasten it to the skirting board with a cable staple. If you are running cable that does not have connectors attached, you only need to drill a hole slightly bigger than the diameter of the cable and about a centimetre in diameter. If you have the connector attached, you need to drill a hole about 1.5 cm in diameter.

1 Use a drill bit slightly larger than the diameter of your Ethernet cable and approximately 1 cm in diameter.

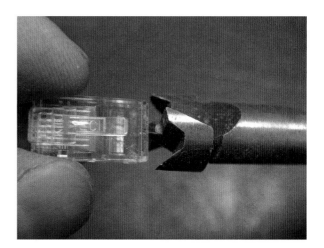

2 Drill a hole between the walls or floor that separate the rooms of your house between which you want to run the cable. If you can go through a cupboard or lift up a skirting board and drill behind it, so much the better because it will be easier to hide your cable.

HOT TIP: Keep the hole you drill close to the floor so that it's difficult to see, but make it higher or lower than your electrical outlets to minimise the chances of drilling into an electrical line.

3 Walls in adjacent rooms are several inches apart from one another. You'll have to drill two holes. After drilling through the wall in the first room, you'll need to drill a second hole in from the wall in the adjacent room unless your drill bit is long enough to reach through. Drill away, if needed. You can clean up the hole later on and fill it in with joint compound.

4 Pull the cable through the hole using a coat hanger. (In the adjacent image, I have used a coat hanger to pull the Ethernet cable through an air duct.)

5 Run the cable under the cupboard or other door, if necessary. If there isn't enough space between the door and the floor, you'll have to drill a hole in the bottom of the doorjamb to get the cable through.

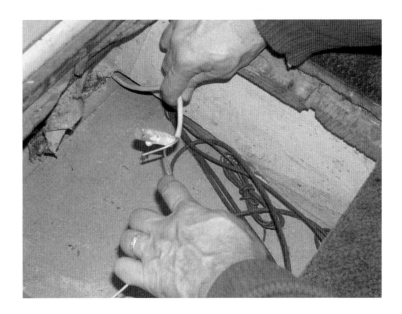

 HOT TIP: To help make sure the holes in adjacent walls line up, measure carefully: if the hole in room A is 15 cm up from the floor and 1 metre from the nearest wall, make sure your hole in room B is also 15 cm up from the floor and 1 metre from the same wall.

 ALERT: Alert: Be sure to measure the distance of your segment before you start fishing the cable through walls, and measure carefully before you cut the cable from the spool.

Run cable between floors

If your computers are in rooms on different floors of your home, or if your router and computers are on different floors, cabling is more difficult. The same principles that apply when you're working on a single floor apply in this situation, too. Use cupboards that are stacked on top of one another if possible; you can also use the holes that have been drilled for radiators or pipes that already run between the rooms.

1 Using a tape measure, measure the distance as closely as you can and make sure that you have enough cable. You'll probably need more than you think because you'll be going between floors and probably can't run the cable in a straight line.

2 If you can't hide the cable in a cupboard, run it in the corner so it can follow the seam in the wall, as shown in the adjacent image.

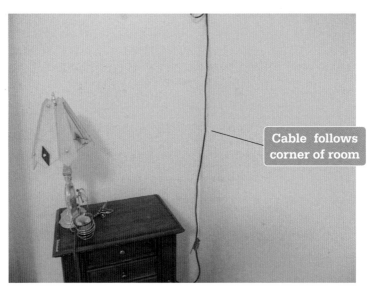

Cable follows corner of room

HOT TIP: Work from the top down rather than the bottom up. That way, you'll use gravity to your advantage when you are running cable from one floor to another.

Fasten cable

So as not to turn your house into a piece of Swiss cheese, there are advantages to running your cable through existing holes alongside other wires. Something as simple as a twist tie is useful to keep your cable from getting tangled. Another trick is to use existing furnishings and features to hide your cable. An obvious example is to lift up the edge of your carpet and run your cable underneath it. Just make sure you don't pierce the cable on any nails or carpet-grabbers underneath.

1 Fasten cable securely to the skirting board or floor with a cable staple.

2 When running cable next to the carpet, try to tuck it under the carpet. You may have to tape it to the floor to keep it fixed.

3 If you already have telephone or other lines running between floors, add the Ethernet cable to them and tie them up with a twist tie or plastic connector.

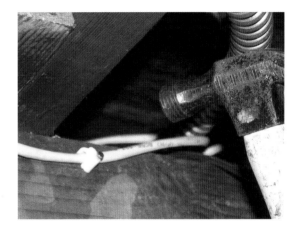

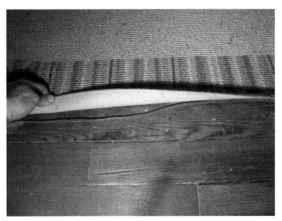

ALERT: When fastening down the staple with the staple gun, be gentle and don't press down too hard or you may damage the cable. Also, line up the cable in between the staple points. Make sure that the points don't pierce the cable.

Add a cable faceplate

A faceplate is a flat plastic fixture that attaches to a wall to cover up an electrical outlet, a phone line or an Ethernet line. Special faceplates are available at hardware stores to accommodate Ethernet cables (don't get the size for phone lines: they're too small). Not only do faceplates look good, but they can shorten the length of Ethernet cable you need to go to a computer or other device. Instead of stretching all the way from one room or one floor to another, you can run the cable to the back of the faceplate, then you only need a length of cable to go from the receptacle on the front of the faceplate to the device.

1 Run your cable through walls or floors and end it at the spot where you want the faceplate to be located.

2 Strip off 2.5 cm of the outer sheath and expose the four twisted pairs of wires, as described earlier in this chapter.

3 Fasten the wires to the screw posts on the back of the faceplate, following the instructions that came with the faceplate.

4 Plug the Ethernet cable into the faceplate and test it out.

> **! ALERT:** Ideally, you want to screw the faceplate into wood, not plaster. You could position your faceplate so it will screw into a stud in the wall, for instance. If you can't find a stud, purchase two plastic anchors: plastic sleeves that are tapered at the end and that have a hole in the centre for a metal screw. You drill a hole into plaster or wallboard, insert the sleeve into the hole, and screw the screw into the sleeve. As the screw goes in, the sleeve expands and fastens itself securely to the wallboard. Such anchors are inexpensive and can be found at any hardware store.

Share your internet connection

One of the most common reasons for configuring a home network is the need to share a single internet connection among two or more computers so that everyone in a family or office can be online at the same time. To share such a connection, the internet Connection Sharing utility needs to be enabled. internet Connection Sharing is built in with Windows 7, so is not something you need to install.

1 Connect one computer to your router, and make sure your router is connected to the internet.

2 Click Start.

3 Click Control Panel.

4 Click the View network status and tasks link, in the Network and internet section.

5 Click Change adapter settings.

6 Right-click the active connection (the one that does not have a red X next to it) and choose Properties from the contextual menu that opens.

7 From the Properties window for your connection that appears, click the Sharing tab.

8 There, select the Allow other network users to connect through this computer's internet connection tick box.

9 Click OK. On the other computer, open a web browser and connect to a website to make sure the connection works.

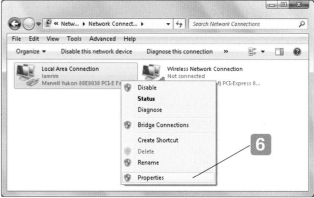

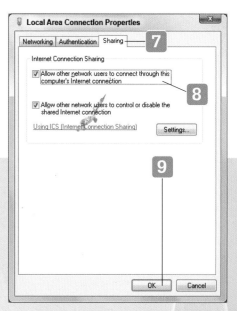

Connect your internet phone

Many internet service providers offer a conventional telephone service (home-based rather than mobile phone) along with a broadband internet connection. The phone service carries a separate fee over and above what you pay for internet access. But the advantage is that by 'bundling' phone and internet, and possibly TV service, you save money overall.

1 Your internet service provider will give you a modem for your phone. This is separate from the modem you use for internet connections. Hook up the modem according to your ISP's instructions.

2 You may need to position the phone modem near your DSL/cable modem and your router so that all three can share the same internet connection. In this image you see, from left to right, a DSL modem, wireless router and DSL phone modem.

3 Connect the modem to your router using a length of Ethernet cable.

? DID YOU KNOW?
You can use a conventional cordless or wired phone with your internet phone. It looks and behaves just like a landline phone.

! ALERT: Some wireless phones have the potential to interfere with a wireless internet connection. Make sure you obtain a phone that uses the 5.8 GHz or higher frequency range. These will not interfere with wireless computer communications.

4 Run a phone line from the phone modem to a wall jack or to the location in your home where you want to place your phone.

5 Plug in your phone to the line with a conventional phone cable. Your ISP may provide you with special phone jack extensions that work with a DSL line if you have one.

? DID YOU KNOW?

When you obtain internet phone service, you gain the ability to track and monitor your phone calls with your computer. Your ISP will provide you with a webpage where messages can be stored and played.

▶ SEE ALSO: See Chapter 9 for more on receiving messages with your internet-based phone.

Dial up to the internet

If your choice is to establish a dial-up internet connection through your internet service provider, you're all set as long as your computer comes with an internal or external modem. First of all, make sure your external modem is turned on before setting up the connection. Also make sure that the phone and the serial or USB cables are connected.

1 Click Start.

2 Click Control Panel.

3 Click Network and internet.

4 Click Network and Sharing Center.

5 Click Set up a new connection or network.

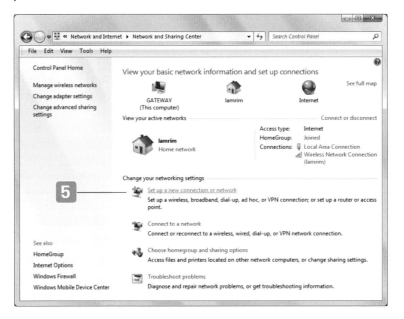

6 Click Connect to the internet.

SEE ALSO: The steps for checking to see if your computer has a built-in modem are virtually the same as checking for a network card. See 'Make sure your computer is internet ready' in Chapter 1, which shows how to check for network hardware. Look under the Modems category for an internal modem.

7 Click Dial-up.

8 Type connection information when prompted, such as your ISP's dial-up phone number. You will also need to type your internet account's user name and password.

9 Click Connect.

10 Once connected, you will see a window labelled The connection to the internet is ready to use. Click Close and start browsing with your web browser or check your email.

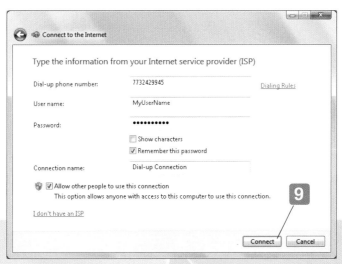

HOT TIP: Select the Remember this password tick box if you want to avoid having to type your password each time you connect.

DID YOU KNOW?
You can tick the Allow other people to use this connection box if you want to share your connection.

Locate a wireless network

Looking for bars in the case of a wireless network isn't the same as trying to find a place to have a drink with a friend! But if you want to use the network to connect with a friend, the more green bars you see, the stronger your signal strength is.

1 Locate the system tray and pass your mouse over the network connection icon.

2 When you see an alert message that indicates that wireless networks are available, single-click the icon and choose Connect to a network.

3 Choose the network to which you want to connect by clicking on it.

4 Click Connect.

ALERT: Take note of whether the wireless network is security enabled or unsecured. If you use an unsecured network, a hacker can use software to steal information off your computer while you work.

3 Starting to use a Web browser

Introduction

Windows 7 comes with Internet Explorer 8, an application you can use to surf the internet. Internet Explorer 8 is a web browser, and it has everything you need, including a pop-up blocker, zoom settings and accessibility options, as well as tools you can use to save your favourite webpages, set home pages, and sign up for read RSS feeds and web slices. Internet Explorer has a feature called tabbed browsing, too – with tabs, you can have multiple webpages open at any one time, without having multiple instances of Internet Explorer open and running. Accelerators are a new feature. When you highlight data on a page, an accelerator icon appears. Click it and you can perform tasks with the selected data, including mapping an address, emailing the link, and more.

Launch Internet Explorer

Internet Explorer 8 (hereafter referred to as IE8) offers all of the tools you'll need to surf the internet. As with other applications, it has toolbars and icons where you can access everything you need to perform internet-related tasks. You can save links to your most often accessed websites, use tabs to open multiple websites at the same time, and type words into a Search window to help you locate anything at all on the Web. There's also RSS for subscribing to websites that offer an RSS feed (which allow you to download only current information for the site, which is often news headlines, new articles, or new travel discounts), and better security than ever. Finally, there are accelerometers, a new way to work with selected data.

1 To open IE8, look for the big blue 'e' on the taskbar. Click once to open the program.

2 When the IE8 window opens, familiarise yourself with the main features. These include but are not limited to:

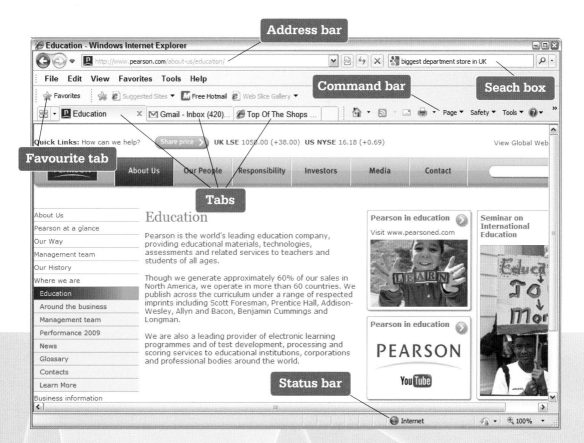

WHAT DOES THIS MEAN?

Address bar: used to type in internet addresses, also known as URLs (universal resource locators). Generally, an internet address takes the form of http://www.companyname.com.

Command bar: used to access icons such as the Home and Print icons. See Table 1 for a list of icons and their uses.

Tabs: used to access websites when multiple sites are open.

Search box: used to search for anything on the internet.

Status bar: used to find information about the current activity.

Favourites tab: used to access your list of saved websites, called Favourites.

 **DID YOU KNOW?**

Because IE8 uses new technologies for obtaining web data, if you come across a website that does not look or 'act' the way you think it should, you can click Compatibility View Settings under the Tools menu, which should correct obvious flaws in appearance or funtionality.

 HOT TIP: You can also open Internet Explorer from the Start menu, from the All Programs list. It's at the top.

Navigate to a website

Your first order of business is to type in a URL and go to a website. URLs and website names (as far as we're concerned just now) start with http://www. I don't want to go into detail about why this is, but suffice it to say, in almost all instances you'll need to type the www. part first. After the www., you'll type the website's name. Often this is the name of the company, such as Amazon or Microsoft, and its ending, which is often .com, .edu, .gov, .org, or .net.

1 Click once in the Internet Explorer address box. Any text that is currently in the box will be highlighted so that you can type over it.

2 Type the URL of a website you want to visit and press Enter.

 HOT TIP: Just because your software may come with a web browser doesn't mean you have to use the same one all the time. I'm partial to Firefox. To download and install it, go to www.mozilla.org.

? DID YOU KNOW?

.com is the most popular website ending – it means the website is a company, business, or personal site. .edu is used for educational institutions, .gov for government entities, .org for non-profit organisations (mostly), and .net for miscellaneous businesses and companies, or personal websites. There are others though, including .info, .biz, .tv, and .uk.com.

? DID YOU KNOW?

When a website name starts with https://, it means it's secure. When purchasing items online, make sure the payment pages have this prefix.

WHAT DOES THIS MEAN?

Home page: The webpage that opens when you open IE8. You can set the home page and configure additional pages to open as well.

Load: A webpage must 'load' before you can access it. Some pages load instantly while others take a few seconds.

Navigate: The process of moving from one webpage to another or viewing items on a single webpage. Often the term is used as follows: 'Click the link to navigate to the new webpage.'

Website: A group of webpages that contains related information. Microsoft's website has information about Microsoft products, for instance.

URL: The information you type to access a website, such as http://www.microsoft.com.

Choose a home page for your browser

What image do you want to greet you when you start up your computer? Maybe you want to gaze upon images of your loved ones. Maybe you want to get right down to business with a page that lets you search the Web (such as Google, http://www.google.co.uk). When you decide, follow the steps below.

1 Visit the page that you have chosen as your home page.

2 Look for the icon in the IE8 command bar that resembles a house. Click the down arrow next to the home icon.

3 Click Add or Change Home Page.

4 Review the What Does This Mean? section below. Then select one of the options provided.

5 Click Yes.

ALERT: Double check before you make your choice. Verify that the webpage you want really is the one that is currently displayed in your browser window. Then go ahead and designate it as your home page.

WHAT DOES THIS MEAN?

There's no harm here in having commitment issues. If you want only one home page, select 'Use this webpage as your only home page'. But if there are multiple home pages you like and you just can't choose, select 'Add this webpage to your home page tabs'. And there is yet another way to go. If you have multiple tabs open in the current browser window and you want them all to function as home pages, choose 'Use the current tab set as your home page'.

Search for information online

If you know the address of the website you want to visit, you can type it into the address bar at the top of the browser window and be there before you can swallow your next sip of coffee. But what about if you're looking for a topic or want to find information without knowing the exact site? If you follow the directions below, you probably won't be able to drink your whole cup of coffee before you get there.

1 Type the topic or phrase in the search bar in the upper-right corner of the browser window.

2 Click the magnifying glass icon or press the Enter key. You'll see your results in the browser window.

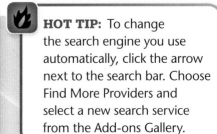

3 If you want to search text within the browser page, click the arrow and select Find on this Page. Then you can search the text of your open page for keywords or phrases.

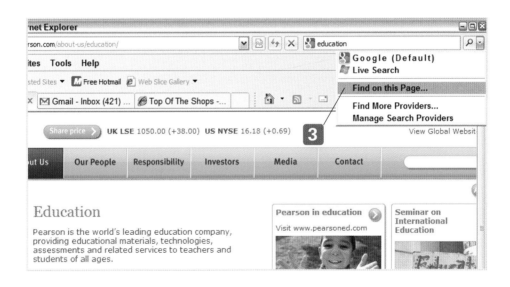

Visit more than one website at a time

You may not notice it at first, but your window will display tabs just above a website's URL. If the tab is long, it's the site that is open. If the tab is smaller, it's a link to open other tabs.

1 Click the smaller tab to open another tab in the same browser window.

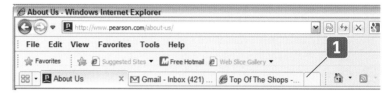

2 When the blank browser window opens, you can type another address in the address bar to open another site.

3 Keep clicking the smaller tabs to open more tabs.

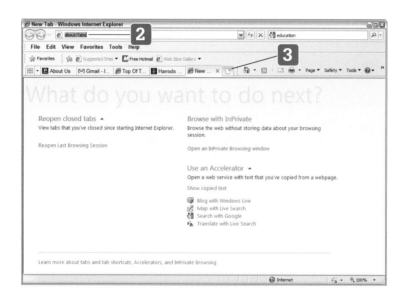

? DID YOU KNOW?
You can switch between tabs by clicking the tab you want. The other tabs won't close, but the focus of the browser will switch to the active tab. When you are ready to close a tab, click the X to the right of the name. The browser itself will stay open.

🔥 HOT TIP: The advantage of using tabs is that you don't have to clutter your workspace by having multiple windows open at one time. You can reorder the way they are laid out by clicking and dragging them within your browser window.

Make pages more readable

Sometimes it's a matter of personal preference. People get attached to fonts the same way they like a particular brand of tea. But type sizes can be easier on the eyes if they are a little larger. Here's how to personalise your browser's settings so that webpage text will be easier to read.

1 Click Page.

2 When the menu appears, scroll down to Text Size. This time I'm saying 'scroll' because I mean it: clicking won't work.

3 The submenu will appear. Then slide your mouse pointer straight to the left so you can choose one of the text size options.

4 To make things bigger, click Page and click Zoom. That will enlarge not only the text but all content on the page.

5 Choose a Zoom option. The default is 100%, but you can specify whatever you want.

? DID YOU KNOW?

If text is formatted on a webpage as a graphic image, it will stay the same size no matter what you do. It won't be enlarged if you change text settings in your browser.

Mark a page so you can revisit it

If you go often to a webpage, you can get there quickly as well by designating it as a 'favourite'. It will save you time and hassle.

1 Determine which webpage you want to designate as a favourite. Navigate there the old-fashioned way for the last time.

2 Look for the icon that looks like two stars. That's the Add to Favourites icon. Click on it.

3 Choose Add to Favourites.

4 Pick a name for the website and type it in.

5 Click Add.

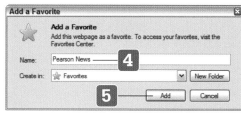

Revisit a favourite webpage

If you look next to the Add to Favourites icon, you'll see a single star. That's the icon that opens the Favourites Center. This is where you view and organise the pages you have saved. But what if you want to go back to a page but can't remember the address? There's also a history of webpages you have visited recently, which you will find very useful.

1 Click the Favourites Center icon when you want to revisit a page.

2 Open a folder. That's where you'll find a page you have saved as a favourite.

3 For instant access to a page, just click.

4 Then click the down arrow that you'll find next to History.

5 Click the date when you previously visited a page.

6 Click the page you want to revisit.

 HOT TIP: You can also press Alt+C to open the Favourites Center. Just make sure that you're online first.

Create a Favourites folder

If you get carried away and start to save a lot of favourite pages, you'll soon find yourself with a very long list. That's when it's time to organise. Just like with your filing cabinet in your home office, the solution is a set of folders. When you store your favourite pages in folders, you can find them conveniently.

1 Click Add to Favourites.

2 Choose Organize Favourites.

3 Click New Folder.

4 Think of a name for your folder, type it, and press Enter.

5 Click a page you want to file. Click Move. Then choose a folder so you can move the page into it.

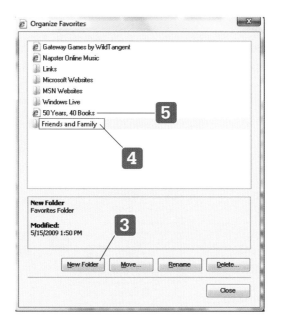

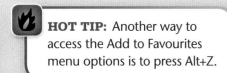 **HOT TIP:** Another way to access the Add to Favourites menu options is to press Alt+Z.

HOT TIP: Maybe you were planning a trip, so you added a lot of travel sites to your Favourites folders. Now the trip is over, so it's time to clean up. From time to time, delete pages you don't care about any more. That way they won't clutter up your Favourites folders.

Block distracting pop-ups

Sometimes you want them, but other times you don't. What are they? A pop-up is a webpage that appears while you are viewing another webpage. A pop-up may be because of something you've done. Maybe you've clicked a link on a page or a remote site received your information when you filled out a form. Or you may get an advertisement because you've merely visited a webpage which causes an advertisement to appear. Here's how to get rid of those you don't want but keep those that are of interest to you.

1 Open Internet Explorer.

2 Click Tools.

3 Click Pop-up Blocker.

4 Choose Turn On (or Turn Off) Pop-up Blocker if needed.

5 Choose Pop-up Blocker Settings if you want to specify a website that you want to show pop-ups.

6 Type the address of the site.

7 Click Add.

8 Click Close.

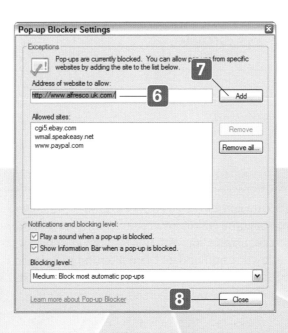

Browse the Web securely

There is, I'm sorry to say, stranger danger on the internet. Viruses, hackers, and dangerous emails are real concerns. But don't panic and run into a corner and hide. There are measures you can take to feel safe and secure as you browse sites, exchange email and shop online.

1 The first step is the most important. Install antivirus software as soon as you set up your computer. Then don't ignore those prompts. Update it on a regular basis.

2 As previously mentioned, look for https: in the address. That means a website is secure and you can submit sensitive information such as credit card numbers with confidence.

3 Never click on a link or open an attachment to an email without knowing that the sender is your friend or a reliable source.

4 Online is not a good place to store information such as your phone number and address. Be sensible about what you reveal to the general public on sites such as Facebook.

5 Leave the campsite clean. Go into a website, do what you need to do, and then sign out when you're leaving.

You are logged in as **gholden**| Log Out |

6 This isn't about stealing, it's about protecting your property. A glass of wine can be really expensive if you spill it on your keyboard. Also keep birds and cats, for example, away from your computer.

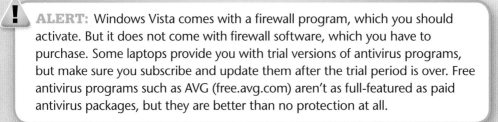

ALERT: Windows Vista comes with a firewall program, which you should activate. But it does not come with firewall software, which you have to purchase. Some laptops provide you with trial versions of antivirus programs, but make sure you subscribe and update them after the trial period is over. Free antivirus programs such as AVG (free.avg.com) aren't as full-featured as paid antivirus packages, but they are better than no protection at all.

Adjust your browser toolbars

There's always a price to pay. If you have a lot of toolbars open, you can do a lot of things. But then you have less room to view webpage content. What are toolbars? They are the areas near the top of an application window that contain tabs, buttons, and other controls. Here's how to control what you see and what you don't.

1 Open Internet Explorer.

2 Click Tools.

3 Click Toolbars.

4 Slide your mouse pointer over to an unticked toolbar to add it to your browser.

5 Slide your mouse pointer over to a ticked toolbar to remove it.

? DID YOU KNOW?

Your Favourites toolbar is one you configure yourself by adding buttons that function as shortcuts to websites you visit a lot. The History toolbar is a little different because it opens and shows websites you have visited recently. In fact, it has its own toolbar. There is also a pane that lists websites with RSS feeds you have subscribed to. The explorer bar is also a pane, this one allowing you to research terms in reference books that are included with Vista.

Erase your browser 'footsteps'

Sometimes you've been there and done that, and you just don't want to retrace your steps. Or, more importantly, maybe you don't want others who use your computer to know where you've been on the internet. Here's how to erase your history as well as other information about your online activities. Doing so is not just a matter of privacy, it can conserve memory on your computer as well.

1 Open Internet Explorer.

2 Press the Alt key on the keyboard.

3 Click Tools.

4 Click Delete Browsing History.

5 Click the Delete button next to the item you want to erase.

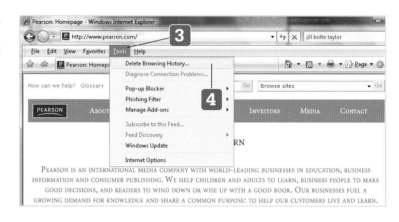

6 Click Delete all to erase all stored information at once.

7 Click Close.

Use accelerometers

One of the most common tasks you'll do in IE8 is to copy data from a webpage. You'll need to copy an address and then paste that address into a mapping website to obtain a route. You'll copy a map and then paste it into an email to send to someone else. You may even copy data from one website, and then go to another to find its meaning. Accelerometers let you perform these most common copy and paste tasks more quickly. There are many accelerometers, and web designers can create their own. To access an accelerometer, highlight any data on a webpage and then click the accelerometer icon.

1 Open any webpage in IE8.

2 Copy any data on the page.

3 Locate the accelerometer icon.

4 Click the accelerometer icon.

5 Click any option. Here I've selected Map with Live Search. Note the map.

6 If desired, click the map for additional directions.

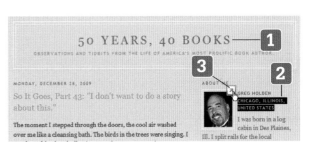

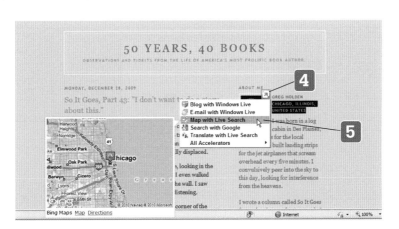

? DID YOU KNOW?

Some of the accelerometers available to you are: Blog with Windows Live; Define with Encarta; E-Mail with Windows Live; Map with Live Search; Search with Live Search; and Translate with Windows Live. Those proficient in web design can even create their own accelerometers.

Print a webpage

Sometimes, it's helpful to print a webpage – for instance, if you get driving directions from a mapping service such as Mapquest (http://www.mapquest.com) and you want to take them with you on the road. Printing features are accessed from the Print icon on the command bar. Clicking the Print icon once will print the page to your computer's default printer.

1 Locate a page on the internet you'd like to print.

2 To print the page without configuring any print options or preferences, click the Print icon.

3 To see how the page will look after it's printed, click the down arrow next to the Print icon and choose Print Preview.

4 If you are happy with the way it looks, click the Print icon. If you do not like the way it appears, click the X in the top right corner to close the window and skip to Step 5.

5 Click the arrow next to the Print icon and click Page Setup.

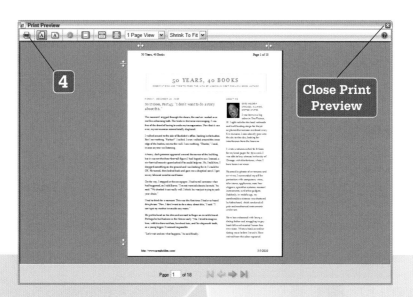

HOT TIP: Clicking the Print icon will take you directly to the Print dialogue box.

6 In the Page Setup dialogue box, make the desired selections.

7 When you've finished, click OK.

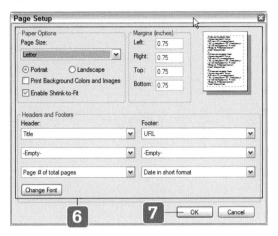

8 Click the arrow next to the Print icon and choose Print.

9 If you have more than one printer, you'll need to choose the printer and set other printer options before clicking Print.

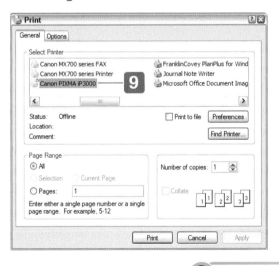

? DID YOU KNOW?

If you click Page Setup, you open the Page Setup dialogue box. Here you can select a paper size and source, and create headers and footers. You can also change orientation and margins, all of which is dependent on what features your printer supports.

? DID YOU KNOW?

Clicking Print Preview opens a window where you can see before you print what the print-out will actually look like. You can switch between portrait and landscape views, access the Page Setup dialogue box, and more.

4 Searching the Web

Introduction

'Go to our website' is pretty much the way information is conveyed today. What you can learn is virtually (no pun intended) unlimited through online searches. Of course, the downside is that there is plenty out there that you really don't want to deal with. This chapter will tell you what you need to know about the many kinds of searches that will give you what you need and not bog you down with what you couldn't care less about.

Explore how search engines work

There's an old saying that it's not what you know, it's how you use it. On the Web, it's not what is out there but how to find it. A search engine is nothing more than a really big database. A program called a spider visits lots of webpages and indexes their contents. When you search for a word or phrase, the search engine scans that database to find results. Here's what to do your first time out.

1 Start up Internet Explorer and go to the most popular search engine. It's called Google, and its URL is www.google.co.uk.

2 Type a keyword or other term into the search box.

3 Specify where you want Google to search: click the web to search the entire World Wide Web, or pages from the UK.

4 Click Google Search or press Enter.

5 When your options appear, click on the most likely one to browse for a particular type of web content.

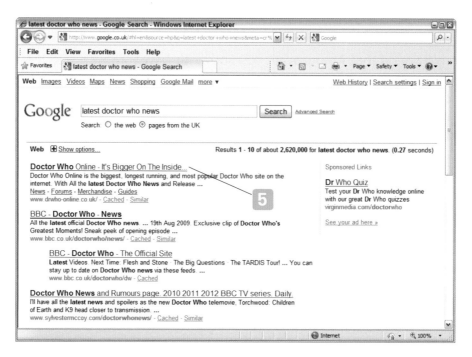

Although Google is the most popular search engine, you have other choices. Some are listed below:

Site	URL
Google	www.google.co.uk
Bing!	www.bing.com
Yahoo!	uk.yahoo.com
Live Search	www.live.com
Ask	uk.ask.com
My Web Search	www.mywebsearch.com

Interpret a page of search results

When you conduct a search on Google or another site, your browser displays a page full of search results. How do you know which one is the most reliable, most impartial, most authoritative, or simply the most relevant? To some extent, you'll have to interpret that by clicking on a site's name and visiting it. But knowing a few search result page characteristics will help you narrow your search.

1 Links off to the side or at the top of a page are sponsored ads: someone has either paid or bid a certain amount to obtain the preferred placement. They aren't necessarily the 'best' sites.

2 You may be able to refine your initial search by clicking on related searches.

3 Scan the complete URLs for a clue as to the source: the link shown here is from the *Daily Telegraph* newspaper.

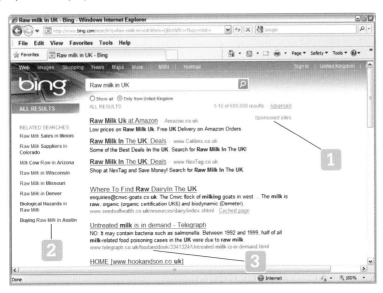

HOT TIP: Read the brief webpage description presented beneath the title of each page. If you see a series of repeated words, these are just words that the site's owner has put on the page simply to get better search placement. Pay attention to the description and see whether it seems relevant before you click.

HOT TIP: If you don't see what you want on the first page of search results, click on subsequent ones. Search engines typically return dozens of pages' worth of results. The first page doesn't always contain the best links.

Browse the Web by category

The Web is so immense, it may help your search to narrow the playing field. Search engines such as Google and Yahoo! also provide you with a categorically organised directory to the Web. As you'd expect, a directory is a list of sites by topic. Here's how to get to one.

1 This time using Yahoo! as an example, type in the following URL: dir.yahoo.com.

2 When the Yahoo! Directory page appears, click on the topic of your choice to find sites that cover it. For this example, click Entertainment.

3 When the Entertainment page appears, enter a search term.

4 Click Category to search only Entertainment-related pages.

5 Click Search.

DID YOU KNOW?

The sites listed in these subject directories are reviewed on a regular basis by employees of the search engine to ensure the quality of the information posted.

Search for an exact phrase

Something is bound to show up, no matter what you type for a search. But you can have a better chance of getting a good match if you refine your searches to get more specific results. You can also restrict your search to a specific website, either by date or by specifying a numeric range if, for example, you're shopping.

1 Navigate to the Google home page.

2 Click Advanced Search.

3 When the Advanced Search page appears, type the exact phrase that you want to be sure will appear in the matching pages.

4 Type up to three words or phrases if you want the matching pages to include one or more of these words or phrases.

5 Type the name of the site you want to search (for instance, Pearson.com).

6 Click Advanced Search.

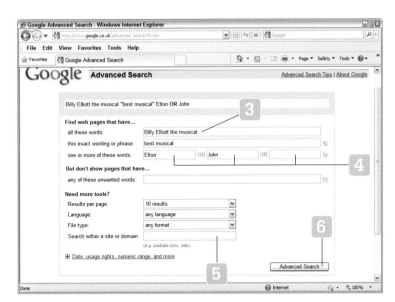

Use an online reference resource

You don't have to search your shelves for a dictionary or thesaurus any more; the weather is available with just a few clicks; so are maps to take you anywhere you can imagine. What's even better is that they are updated constantly so you're never stuck with something that is obsolete.

1 Click on the site's search box to position the cursor there.

2 Convey the information you want to find by typing a word, phrase, or question.

3 Click the Search button.

4 Scan the search results. Some sites, such as Dictionary.com, let you hear the pronunciation of a word by clicking on the speaker icon.

? DID YOU KNOW?

Many reference sources can be searched for free on the internet, but well-known ones like the *Oxford English Dictionary* and *Encyclopaedia Britannica* are not: you have to subscribe to be able to search the online versions of these publications.

Search from your browser's address box

Searching the internet is without a doubt one of the most popular online activities. For this reason, the most popular web browsers have search engine boxes integrated right into their interface. Instead of first going to the search engine site, you can enter the search term within the browser itself.

1 Click in the search box to the right of the address box near the top of the Internet Explorer window. The cursor appears in the box so you can begin typing.

2 Type a word, phrase or question to let the engine know the type of information you want to find.

3 Click the Search button, which looks like a magnifying glass.

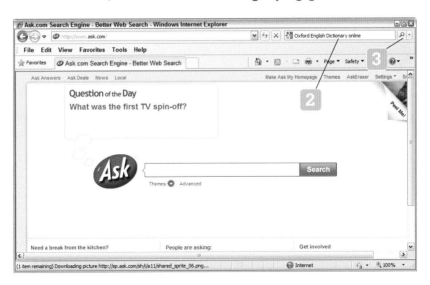

4 To refine your search, click the down arrow next to the Search button.

5 Choose a different search engine.

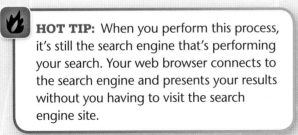

HOT TIP: When you perform this process, it's still the search engine that's performing your search. Your web browser connects to the search engine and presents your results without you having to visit the search engine site.

Set your search preferences

It's all well and good to feel like you have a world of information at your fingertips. But sometimes you're better off with a speciality. Preferences are used to configure your search results by restricting them. Maybe you want to see results only in English. Maybe you don't want explicit text or images. Or maybe you want to set the number of results that will be displayed on each page.

1 Go to the Google home page.

2 Click Search settings.

3 Choose the language you want Google to use.

4 Tick one or more of the boxes beside the language(s) you want to use.

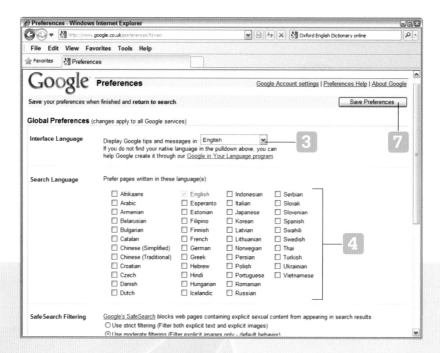

5 Determine whether or not you want filtering. If so, click Use strict filtering. If not, click Do not filter my search results.

6 Click the number of pages you want to see in the results. The default is 10, but you can display up to 100.

7 Click Save Preferences.

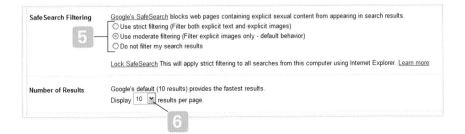

Safe Search Filtering Google's SafeSearch blocks web pages containing explicit sexual content from appearing in search results.
5
○ Use strict filtering (Filter both explicit text and explicit images)
◉ Use moderate filtering (Filter explicit images only - default behavior)
○ Do not filter my search results

Lock SafeSearch This will apply strict filtering to all searches from this computer using Internet Explorer. Learn more

Number of Results Google's default (10 results) provides the fastest results.
Display 10 ▾ results per page.
6

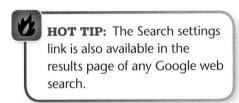

HOT TIP: The Search settings link is also available in the results page of any Google web search.

Consult a Web encyclopedia

Wikipedia is not written by professionals – there are more than 75,000 contributors who between them have written more than 10 million articles, 2.5 million of them in English. You don't always know who has written the information you see there. However, Wikipedia is free, and it's one of the Web's largest reference sites.

1 Type http://en.wikipedia.org/ inside the address bar of your web browser.

2 Press Enter or Return.

3 Use the search box to type a word or phrase that represents the information you want to find.

4 Click Go.

 HOT TIP: If you prefer to browse the Wikipedia articles, click Contents and then use the links to browse articles alphabetically or by category.

? DID YOU KNOW?
Click Search if you want to go through all the Wikipedia content and not just article titles.

Search within a webpage

Getting to a webpage is a good first step. But some pages contain hundreds or even thousands of words. If you're looking for something in particular, it saves a lot of time if you use a word or phrase to cut to the chase.

1 Press Ctrl+ F or click Edit and choose Find on this Page.

2 When the Find bar appears, type your search text.

3 The first match will be displayed, along with the total number of other matches.

4 Click Next to find more matches.

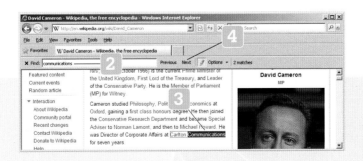

5 Staying safe and secure online

Introduction

Many of the first questions my 80-year-old father asked me about the internet were not about what he could do online but about viruses and other security threats. He had heard the term 'hackers' long before he understood what 'web surfer' meant. There are frequently stories about cyber-wars and the theft of consumers' credit-card data. The good news is that it's a straightforward matter to protect yourself from such dangers and to prevent viruses and other harmful programs from invading your file system. This chapter will make you aware of some simple measures you can take to protect yourself and your computer online.

Understand online threats

When it comes to online security, half of the battle is simply understanding what threats can occur without being fearful of them. Once you understand the ways in which unscrupulous individuals will try to gain access to your computer or your personal information, you'll find it easy to repel them. It's also good to know some security-related terms so you understand them when you see them in the media or online.

1 *Spyware* invades your computer without you even knowing that it's there. A software program will gather your data, steal your passwords, display advertisements, and take control of your web browser. The cure is to install an antispyware or antivirus program.

2 *Phishing attacks* involve fraudulent email messages cleverly designed to look legitimate. The sender induces you to click on a link included with an email message, supposedly to check your credit, or verify your identity. When you click the link, a harmful program is downloaded to your computer. If you fill out a form and submit your personal information such as credit card numbers, your account is robbed. The cure is simply to not click on links from emails sent from strangers.

ALERT: Phishing attacks are especially dangerous. If you click on a link, a harmful program called a Trojan horse can be downloaded to your computer and will perform functions on your machine without your knowledge. Sometimes, hackers take control of computers and turn them into 'zombies'. Once many zombies have been secured, the hacker can get all of them to attack a website at the same time, making it non-functional.

3 Your body doesn't like being sick with a virus, and your computer won't fare any better. A mild case of the computer virus will result in messages you don't want. But other, more severe afflictions result in deleted data, crashes, or even using your computer to attack other computers. An antivirus program like the one shown here will block or remove a virus. Click Scan to manually scan your file system for harmful software.

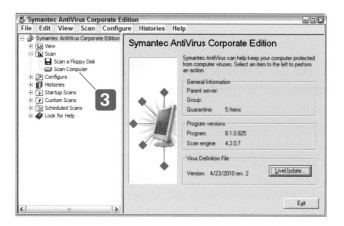

4 Pop-up ads can appear without warning just because you happen to be visiting a certain website. Or you can cause them to appear by taking an action such as clicking a link on a page or submitting information to a remote website by filling out a form. You need to be aware that sometimes if you click items in a pop-up menu you will unknowingly allow spyware or a virus to inhabit your computer. You need to know how to use a pop-up blocker such as the Google toolbar, or a home firewall package.

5 Cookies keep track of your preferences or items you've put into a shopping basket. It's hard to do business with a website store without activating one of these small text files. You should try to tell the site not to save data such as passwords and your credit card information.

Google toolbar with pop-up blocker

6 One secure site indicator is https: and a lock icon in the browser address bar. That means that if you send sensitive data such as your credit card number, the site will use an encrypted format that will make it impossible to read. You need to know when you are filling out a form on an insecure site, because that information will be sent in plain text that anyone can read.

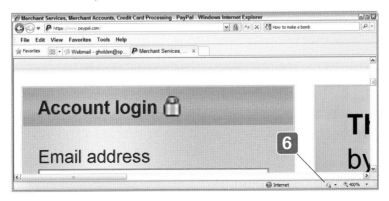

7 A firewall program will monitor suspicious traffic heading into your computer from the internet as well as outbound traffic – from your computer to the internet. Suspicious outbound traffic can occur if a virus or some other harmful program has infected your file system.

HOT TIP: Antivirus and firewall programs work only if they are updated periodically to keep up with the latest threats. When you obtain one, make sure it is set to automatically update itself, or remember to update it manually on a regular basis.

Keep your grandchildren safe

Most children know that if Mum says 'no' they should go and ask Grandma. And I'm not going to discourage you from sneaking an extra edible treat to those little treasures. But as a dad, I am going to ask you point blank to make sure that when your grandchildren visit and ask to use your computer, they don't have access to objectionable material that has been blocked from them at home and school. Even by chance, youngsters can be exposed to inappropriate images, information and chat-room conversations. Don't let it happen on your watch.

1 Unsuitable images can be found on home pages, even if you have to register or pay to get into the site itself. And there are plenty of places to find violent or explicit images for free.

2 People who are up to no good can find plenty of dangerous information online. One problem is profanity and otherwise offensive diatribes. Another problem is obtaining directions on how to harm yourself or others.

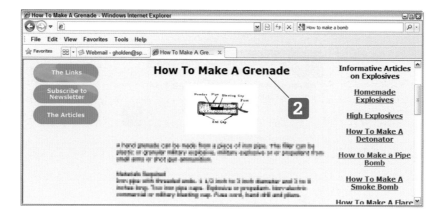

3 Inappropriate chat means stranger danger. Make sure that any child in your care doesn't give out personal details about themselves. Even basic information about where they live or go to school can be used to harm them.

4 Many websites have ratings that allow restrictions unless a user is authorised. If you select Tools, click internet Options, and then click the Content tab, you can use Parental Controls and the Content Advisor.

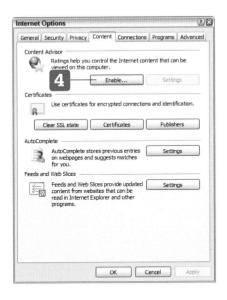

5 Third-party programs have names like CYBERsitter, Net Nanny and Cyberpatrol. They filter out content that is inappropriate for children.

6 Supervision and education can be more powerful than software. Teaching children about problems that they can encounter and giving them rules for using the computer is the first step. But there's no substitute for personal supervision.

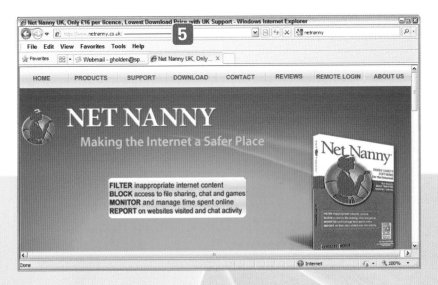

Make sure Windows Firewall is operating

Like fire, many features on the internet can be used for good or evil. It's a good idea to fight fire with fire ... firewall, that is. If you don't want others to join you when you're on your computer, bringing along a virus to add to the party, make sure your firewall is turned on. This usually happens by default, but it's a good idea to check to make sure.

1 Click Start.

2 Click Control Panel.

3 Click Security.

4 Click Windows Firewall.

5 Click Use recommended settings to access the Windows Firewall settings dialogue box.

6 Verify that your computer has turned on Windows Firewall. If not, turn it on right away.

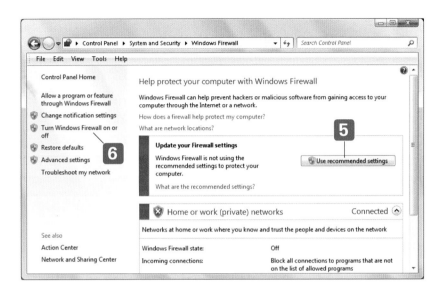

? DID YOU KNOW?

A firewall is different from an antivirus program. An antivirus program continually scans your email and computer for harmful software. A firewall monitors connection attempts that match patterns typically used by hackers. Although these two programs are separate, they can be purchased in a single package, such as Norton Internet Security (www.symantec.com).

Adjust your firewall's settings

Step number one is to reassure yourself that Windows Firewall is up and running. But you may want to go a step further. There are various settings you can change to make your firewall fit your security needs. But first, see which options are active so you can decide whether or not you want to make adjustments.

1 Click Start, then Control Panel, then Security, and then Windows Firewall.

2 Verify that your computer's default feature has turned on Windows Firewall. If not, turn it on by clicking Turn Windows Firewall on or off.

3 Click Turn on Windows Firewall.

4 Click OK.

5 To access programs that can make connections through the firewall, click the Exceptions tab.

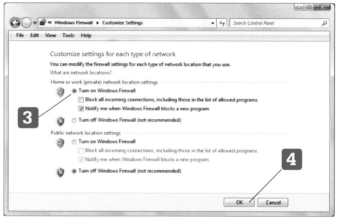

6 Tick the box next to any applications you want to allow through the firewall; untick applications you want to block.

7 Click Add Program to add applications that aren't on Windows Firewall's list.

8 Click OK when you've finished.

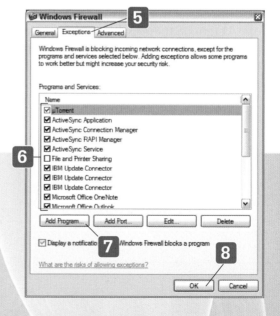

Install and use an antivirus program

Many of the processes and procedures described in this book aim to protect your secure information. However, another sad but true aspect of security has to do with damage. Some potentially dangerous programs (which are called viruses, worms, Trojan horses, rootkits, and the like) are called malicious because they are potentially harmful. They could infect your computer, compromise its operation, and damage or erase folders and files. Here's how to make sure they don't.

1 Open the program you will use for this process so you have access to its features.

2 Review any potential problems that are displayed and decide how to approach the actions required.

3 Perform a scan for viruses by clicking on the Scan button (or Scan Computer).

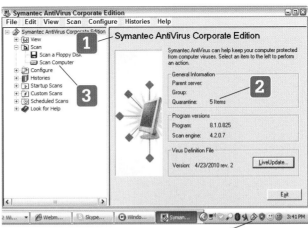

Many anti-virus programs can be opened from the system tray

4 Select the area you want to scan. Selecting the letter assigned to your computer's hard disk (usually this is drive C) will effectively scan your file system. If, however, you have other disk drives present, you may want to scan them as well.

5 Click Scan.

? DID YOU KNOW?

Your antivirus program will also tell you when networks or other types of programs on the internet are trying to get into your computer. You can then decide how to respond to the request for access.

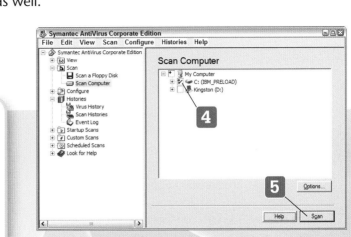

6 Keep track of progress and any problems that are found by making note of any viruses or other suspicious programs that are reported.

7 If viruses are identified, click on the Update button to get the virus definitions. These are the means to stop them, and you can usually set the updates to be performed automatically.

8 Wait for the message announcing that a successful scan has been completed and click Close results (or a similarly named button).

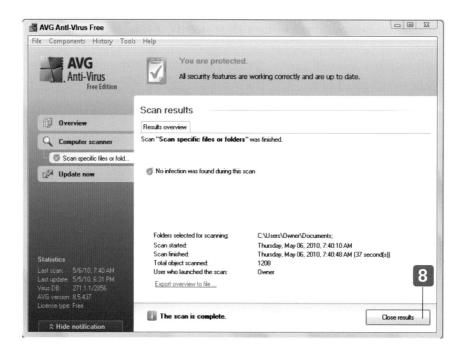

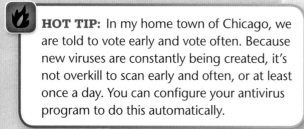

HOT TIP: In my home town of Chicago, we are told to vote early and vote often. Because new viruses are constantly being created, it's not overkill to scan early and often, or at least once a day. You can configure your antivirus program to do this automatically.

Use Windows Defender

The old saying that what you don't know can't hurt you doesn't apply to spyware. This software not only can enter your computer from the internet but also can potentially send your information over the internet. Luckily, a built-in program called Windows Defender can scan your system for spyware and remove it.

1 Click Start.

2 Type defender in the Start box.

3 Click Windows Defender.

4 Review the details displayed in the Windows Defender window for scanning your computer and viewing the results.

5 Begin a scan of your computer by clicking on the Scan button.

6 Wait for the message announcing that no unwanted or harmful software has been detected and your computer is running normally.

7 Click on the Tools button.

8 Click on the Options link.

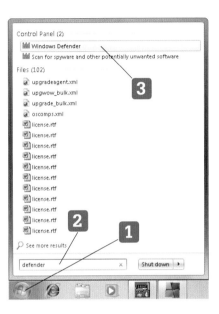

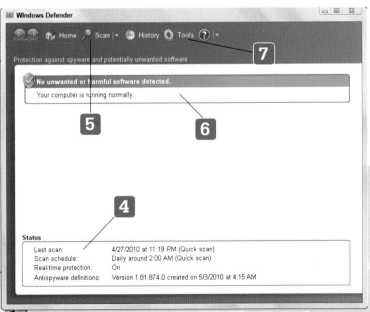

? **DID YOU KNOW?**

If you have a separate antivirus program installed, it will also tell you when networks or other types of programs on the internet are trying to get into your computer. You can then decide how to respond to the request for access.

9 Decide how you want Windows Defender to run and set those options.

10 Return to the Windows Defender window by clicking on the Save button.

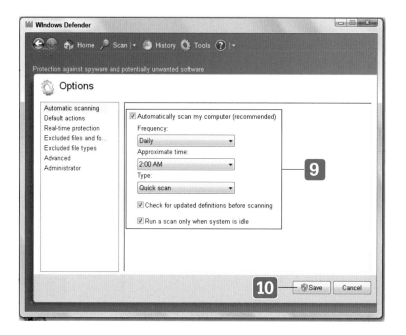

Configure user account controls

The thing about control is that you can be in charge. That means you can run your antivirus programs when you choose and prevent the warning windows from being annoying or interfering with your work. But other warnings that Windows 7 gives you have little to do with viruses or external threats. They're intended to help you monitor your own changes to the system, and you can turn them on or off by following these steps.

1 Click Start and click Control Panel.

2 Click User Accounts and Family Safety.

3 Click on the User Accounts link.

4 Click Change User Account Control settings.

5 Move the slider down to Never notify.

6 Click OK and restart your computer.

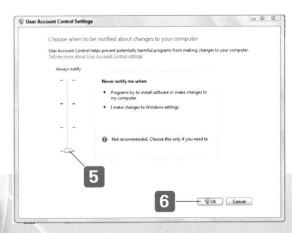

? DID YOU KNOW?

By default, you will find the box ticked that reads Use User Account Control (UAC) to help protect your computer. By performing the tasks in this section, you are overriding a built-in protection.

Check the Security Center

As the name implies, there is a place on your computer that's a clearinghouse of sorts for all your security features. All the settings on your computer are visible in this one location. Not only can you see them, you can also go here to alter the settings of your choice.

1 Click Start and click Control Panel.

2 Click System and Security.

3 Click Action Center.

4 Review the current essential security settings that are displayed.

5 If you want to view the settings for a particular item, click on the box next to it.

6 If you need to alter the settings in the Security Center, click one of the blue highlighted links.

System and Security — **2**
Review your computer's status
Back up your computer
Find and fix problems

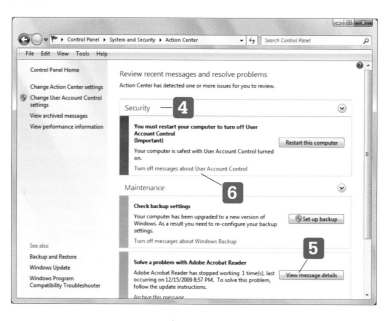

? DID YOU KNOW?

This is pretty obvious, but it's also a pretty good system. Look at the colour of the banner displayed in the Security Center window to assess your current security status – green: this item is fully protected and up to date; yellow: take another look to determine whether there are issues that are compromising this item; red: the required settings are missing and there could be trouble ahead for your computer.

Set your browser's security level

It seems like there's always a trade-off. If you like your web sessions to be super interesting and very interactive, you have your pick of a vast array of webpages with small programs, scripts and other forms of active content. But you will have to pay a big price for your pleasure if this program, which is your primary interface to the internet, turns out to be a portal for bad things that can harm your files. When you set your security level high, you can run only less active content. The choice is yours.

1 Start up IE8.

2 Click Tools.

3 Click internet Options.

4 Click the Security tab.

5 Click internet.

6 Click and drag the Security level for this zone slider to the level you want.

7 Click OK.

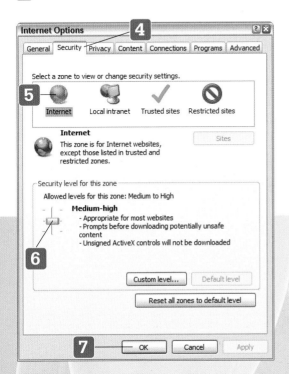

? DID YOU KNOW?

If you trust a website, you can use the Medium security level for it. Instead of clicking internet, click Trusted sites, click Sites, type the address, and click Add.

Protect your identity

You've heard that there's a sucker born every day. But for modern scam artists, there's a potential victim created every time a computer is sold. Identity theft is a real threat, and you don't need me to tell you that it will be a real nightmare if it happens to you. I'd rather spend my time telling you how to protect yourself so that your sensitive information remains yours and yours alone.

1 Think twice before you print off sensitive information from the internet. For one thing, you help the environment by using less paper. For another thing, you don't have a paper trail that can lead to trouble if it falls into the wrong hands. If you do have such papers, shred them on a regular basis – don't just throw them into the rubbish where they can be retrieved and misused.

2 Credit-reporting agencies such as www.equifax.com or www.experian.com can be used to ensure there's no mischief afoot. Make sure no new accounts have been set up in your name and that your credit rating isn't plunging because someone is racking up huge debts in your name.

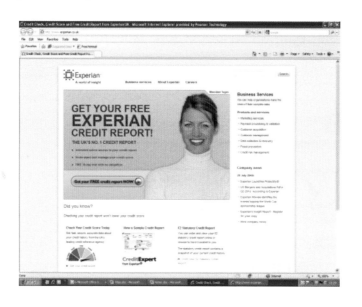

? DID YOU KNOW?

Legitimate sites will have https: in the URL and will cause a lock icon to be displayed in IE8's status bar. They will also have the correct domain name.

3 Go to OptOutPrescreen.com to stop credit card and insurance companies from sending preapproved offers through the mail. If an identity thief gets hold of them, they may have a portal to information they can use.

4 Don't respond to email with links to pages that ask for financial data or your passwords. A process called *phishing* creates replicas of existing websites to fool you into submitting data. That information is then sent directly to the scammer.

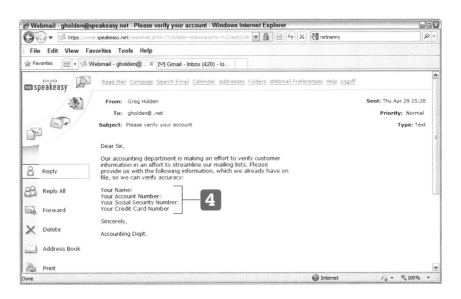

 HOT TIP: To turn on the phishing filter, click Tools, click Phishing Filter, and then click Turn On Automatic Website Checking. Don't do anything on the site if Suspicious Website appears in the address bar.

Clear your browser history

The good thing about a folder called Temporary internet Files is that you can reload favourite websites much quicker because it stores copies of page text, images, and other content. But it also can be a little like hanging your dirty laundry on the clothes line outside where all the neighbours can see. Here's how to keep other people's noses out of your business.

1 Open IE8 and click Tools.

2 Click internet Options.

3 In the General tab, click Delete under Browsing history.

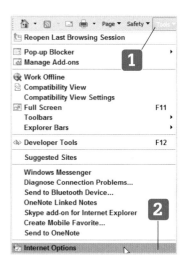

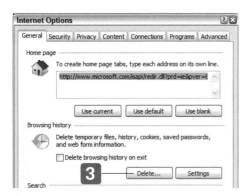

4 Tick the box next to History, and next to any other items you want to delete.

5 Click Delete.

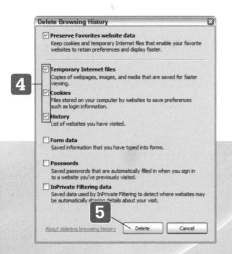

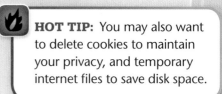

HOT TIP: You may also want to delete cookies to maintain your privacy, and temporary internet files to save disk space.

6 Doing everyday tasks the internet way

Introduction

I know what you're thinking: I'm used to writing letters and paying my bills with a cheque that I drop in the post. Why should I start writing emails and paying bills online? We're all creatures of habit, and there's no reason to change all your habits at once. The internet just provides you with new options. If you try out some of those options or simply learn what they are, you may just find you like doing things the new way – the internet way. This chapter describes some of the many everyday tasks you can accomplish online, and how you can save time – and occasionally money – with just a few mouse clicks.

Make an online purchase

Going to a bricks-and-mortar store is not always necessary any more. Think about it. On days when the weather is bad or you're not able to get out, you can comparison shop all you like from the comfort of your home. You have an endless array of merchandise and services. Your purchase is promptly delivered right to your doorstep. What's not to love?

1 Find a site you like and register, if prompted to do so. You'll find a list of online stores in the UK at http://www.topoftheshops.co.uk.

Click here to register for an account

2 Browse all you like until you've picked out the goods you wish to purchase.

3 Place your selections in a shopping basket by clicking a button next to the item labelled 'Add to Cart' or 'Add to Basket', for instance.

4 Review what you have in your basket, delete any items you don't want, and proceed to the checkout.

5 Enter your shipping information and make your payment.

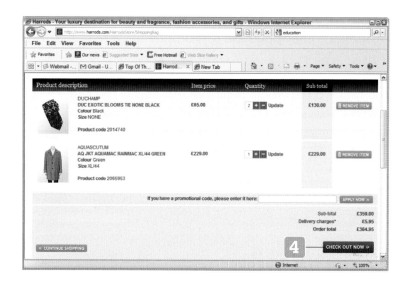

HOT TIP: You can even shop for groceries online. Supermarkets such as Tesco, Safeway and Sainsbury's have websites where you can make purchases and have food delivered to you. You'll find a list of online supermarkets at http://www.somucheasier.co.uk/ supermarkets-uk.html.

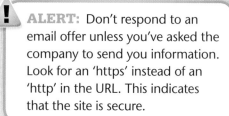

ALERT: Don't respond to an email offer unless you've asked the company to send you information. Look for an 'https' instead of an 'http' in the URL. This indicates that the site is secure.

Find travel deals

I love to travel, and I really love travel brochures. In fact, I've written guidebooks touting my personal favourites. But for heavy-duty research to find the really hidden treasures, there's nothing like the internet. You'll find the latest details and deals online. Many airlines actually charge a fee if you book over the phone and do *not* use the Web. And the world is rapidly becoming ticketless. Whether you need transportation, lodging, dining or a fabulous tourist trap, sooner or later you're going to have to navigate websites. Here's how.

1 Find a site that offers a full travel service or a site for an individual vendor. Some sites, such as the one shown here, offer speciality travel experiences.

2 Select your holiday requirements.

3 Enter dates or other details, for example for a flight or a room.

4 Click on the search button.

HOT TIP: The *Times Online* website regularly reviews UK-based travel websites. You can find a recent review at http://www.timesonline.co.uk/tol/travel/news/article1554167.ece.

HOT TIP: Don't assume that a package deal is the best price. In some cases you'll save money and have more flexibility if you purchase different elements of a holiday from different sites.

Trace your family roots

I love sifting through dusty files in libraries and records offices. I've even been known to tramp around cemeteries. But it's great to get a head start on where to look for that marriage, birth or death certificate. Not only that, but records have been digitised. It's really a very exciting process.

1 Choose a genealogy site like the one shown here and register, if prompted.

2 Enter the details of the family members in the search boxes, or click on links to find specific information.

3 Enter a family name and click on the search button.

4 Find clues in the results that are displayed, and repeat the previous steps.

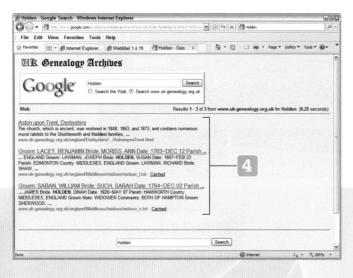

> **HOT TIP:** In addition to the obvious, don't forget that there are lots of different types of records. If one kind was lost in a fire or flood, maybe you can get information another way. Check out records pertaining to the military, census, professional associations, court proceedings, and baptism or church membership.

Read news on the Web

Maybe you can't imagine starting your day without your newspaper in one hand and your cup of coffee in the other. As a former reporter, I'm all for promoting subscriptions. But maybe you want the latest details without waiting for the next morning. Maybe you have a particular interest or cause that you want to read about. Now there are a lot of sources of news and opinion that are never printed.

1. Find a media site, e-zine, blog or news portal.

2. Register, if prompted.

3. Type in a keyword.

4. Keep clicking for more details about that story, or click on other links to find information on other topics.

HOT TIP: An aggregator is a feature that displays syndicated content. Instead of surfing to a web media site or news portal, you can have articles and news headlines sent to you.

Socialise on the Web

Just because you can't see or hear someone doesn't mean you can't get to know them. If you're the talking type, you can participate in chat rooms and discussion boards on every topic you can think of. If you want to meet people who share a common interest, you can exchange information on, for example, books and gardens. And, of course, there's the possibility of finding a pen pal, friend or date.

1. Find a website that covers your local area or a topic of interest. The one shown here presents news and events in the Bristol area.

2. Click on a link for a topic or activity that interests you.

3. Search for a topic by entering a keyword or phrase and pressing Search.

4. Look for links that give you a chance to interact with other residents. This link takes you to a blog written about a local topic.

Have Your Say
Publish your thoughts on the Internet and have your say on blogger.com - here's one readers story - Ban Tankers in North West Bristol

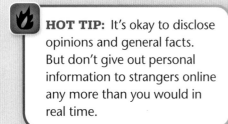

HOT TIP: It's okay to disclose opinions and general facts. But don't give out personal information to strangers online any more than you would in real time.

Play games online

There's a store near me called Marbles which claims you can keep and enhance your mental agility by playing games. We're talking action, sports, puzzle, arcade, board, word, and more. Online you can compete one on one, join a team, or be perfectly content with endless games of Solitaire. Let the games begin!

1 Find an online site that lets you play a game with others who are online and that doesn't charge you anything to join (or that at least charges a reasonable fee). The BBC provides games such as Jeopardy for children of all ages at www.links4kids.co.uk.

2 Choose the type of game you want to play.

- MMOG stands for massively multiplayer online game. A large number of players compete against and with each other.

- A variation of an MMOG is an MMORPG (massively multiplayer online role-playing game). Each player assumes a character and together there is lots of action and drama.

- MUD (multi-user domain [or dungeon]) players also usually assume a role to play the game. But in this case prompts are given to the characters so they can react to and move around a simulated fantasy world.

- Interactive fiction also takes place in a text-based fantasy world. But here there is only one player. You read about your choices and what happens next is determined by what you decide to do. Usually you're trying to solve a puzzle or meet some other goal.

3 Some simple games can be played online by yourself. The *Daily SuDoku*, for instance, offers a daily Sudoku puzzle at www.dailysudoku.com/sudoku/today/shtml. Click in a square and press a number key to add it to the grid.

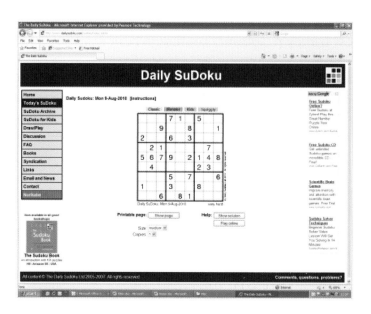

 ALERT: Read the terms and conditions before you sign up for an online game. Some sites require you to purchase tickets to participate. When you register, you may be asked for personal information such as your date of birth, mobile phone number and address. If you don't want to provide so much information, look for another site that is less intrusive.

HOT TIP: Some games have interactive features that require you to download an add-on piece of software called a plug-in that works with Internet Explorer. Of course, there are plenty of games online that don't involve plug-ins. Even a lot of the plug-ins are free. But it may be worth it to pay for a game or to pay the fee to access the gaming site. It really is a lot of fun.

Pay your bills on the Web

Save a stamp ... pay your bill online. That is a win win. Your vendor gets their money promptly, you get a record of the transaction. No lines at the bank or the post office. And when it comes to investing, you can research before you decide and then track the results. There's even the possibility of saving a lot on brokerage fees and trade commissions. You'll need to set up an account with your bank so you can track your accounts online, but your bank's customer service staff will help you do so.

1 Find the site that offers the type of business you wish to conduct. Many financial institutions, including banks, let you pay bills online along with your other services.

2 Ask your institution how to pay bills online, or go to its website, log in with your account information, and click a tab such as Bill Payer or Pay My Bills.

3 For this example (your financial institution's steps will differ), click payments, click Add Payee, click Another Business, and click continue.

> **? DID YOU KNOW?**
>
> Once you are able to access your financial institution's website, you can track your balances and transfer funds from one account to another online.

> **! ALERT:** Be aware of how long it takes to process your payment. Don't pay the same day the bill is due if it will take a day or two to process the transaction.

4 Enter the account number, your name, and other required information for the bill you want to pay.

5 Click Pay Bill, enter the amount you want to pay, and click Pay (or something similar).

6 Print out a copy of the transaction for your paper files.

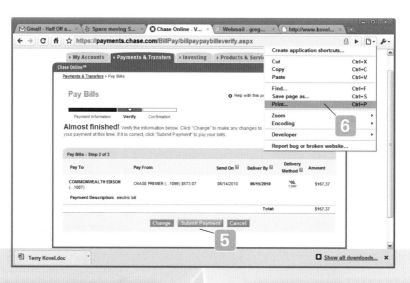

HOT TIP: Beware of emails that tell you there's a problem with your account. If you provide your bank login data, you are likely to be the victim of a scam.

ALERT: Make sure you know whether or not your financial institution will charge you a fee for bill payments. Most do not.

Find a job on the Web

Job sharing, seasonal work, and part-time employment are becoming the norm these days. Working from home isn't just for freelancers. But whether you want speciality employment or a full-time, benefits-eligible profession, online is the place to go.

1 Obtain advice on a general site to update your CV, hone your interview skills, and find out why networking is important.

2 Find out which skills you should tout to prospective employers by doing some aptitude testing.

3 Research occupations to find out what credentials are required, what the job descriptions are, salary scales, and whether the field is hiring.

4 Post your CV and profile on employer sites, job boards, and social networking groups. To post your CV on one of the largest job sites, Monster.com (www.monster.co.uk), click Profile & CV and choose CV from the drop-down list. Follow the steps shown on subsequent screens to post your CV. You'll need to set up an account with Monster.com to follow these steps.

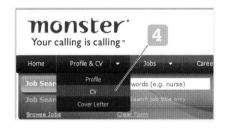

5 Search for jobs on one of the many UK-based employment sites. Directgov (http://jobseekers.direct.gov.uk) offers public service jobs. Enter a keyword in the search box and click Search.

6 You can also click one of the popular searches if one matches the kind of job you are seeking.

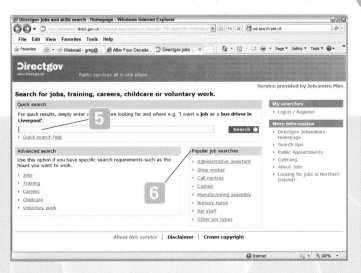

? DID YOU KNOW?

Virtually all online employment sites let you browse through job categories to find the type of position that matches your qualifications. On the Directgov site shown here, click Jobs under the heading Advanced search to click through job categories that include Food, drink & hotels, Manufacturing, and Construction, among others.

Explore sites for silver surfers

It can be difficult to get out to senior centres and activity centres that cater especially to the over-50 population. Even if a centre is available in your town, the prospect of going there alone and attending activities without knowing anyone can be intimidating. But in the comfort of your home, you can find out about medical care, travel opportunities and activities available to people just like you by visiting websites that specialise in this area.

1 Start up IE8 and go to a site such as SilverSurfers.net (www.silversurfers.net).

2 Click on an area of interest you want to explore – in this example, Motorhomes.

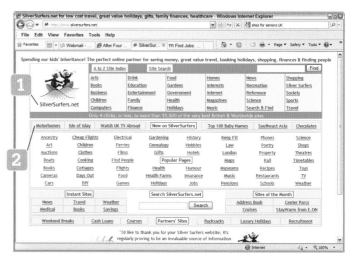

3 Click on links that progressively grow more specific until you find what interests you – for instance, the Camping and Caravanning Club (http://www.campingandcaravanningclub.co.uk).

HOT TIP: Also visit the Seniors page run by TheBigProject.co.uk: http://www.thebigproject.co.uk/links_seniors.htm.

Create your own website

You don't need to be a CEO of a multi-million-dollar corporation to have your own website. Maybe you belong to an organisation with a cause to promote. You may want to create a site to document your family's history. Or maybe you just want to take your grandparents' brag book to a higher level.

1 Choose a topic based on family, personal or professional interests.

2 Find a site that will let you create a website for free using your web browser, such as Spanglefish (www.spanglefish.com). Provide your name, email address, country and company information if applicable. Then click the OK. Sign me up button.

3 This particular site asks you to specify your location and explain your reasons for setting up a website that it will host. Enter this information as well as a password you will use to access your site, and click Finish. Wait for an email giving you access to your site.

4 Watch your limit on memory used to store your files, keeping in mind that usually the more you pay a host, the more storage space you acquire.

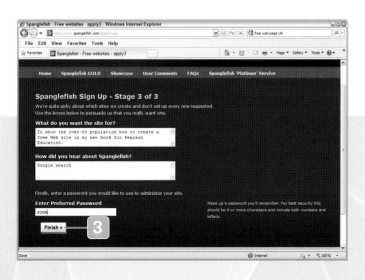

HOT TIP: When deciding on a web-hosting provider, do research on the amount of time it is up and serving and its percentage of downtime. Find out when tech support is available to you and whether it's free. Determine whether you can get such advanced features as forms which let visitors submit information by filling out boxes and clicking option buttons. Also look into how many email accounts are provided.

7 Enjoying entertainment on the internet

Introduction

Maybe you're kicking yourself for falling asleep during the television episode you'd been looking forward to all week. Maybe you were beside yourself with grief when your favourite radio or TV show went off the air. Or perhaps you miss the days of Old Time Radio and want to hear the shows from your childhood once again. Read this chapter to discover some new options on the internet to supplement those in the traditional entertainment world. And when you agree that these are pretty good options, read on to find out how to personalise your fun even more – with you as the star.

Download a song

Reading this chapter will be much more enjoyable if there's some mood music in the background, don't you think? If it's music you've selected, that will be especially good. And where do you find good music these days? You can probably guess the answer by this time. If you haven't noticed, the number of old-fashioned record stores in your area is dwindling. One reason: more and more people are downloading music from the internet and playing it on computers or portable media players such as the popular iPod.

1 Subscribe to an online music service so you can download and play songs. One of the most popular is Amazon (www.amazon.co.uk). Go to the site, pass your mouse pointer over the Music, DVD & Games link, and choose MP3 Downloads.

2 Browse to a song or album you like and click it so its own product page appears. Click Add to Shopping Basket to reserve the entire item (an album or CD) for purchase.

3 Click Add to add a single track on the CD to your shopping basket.

4 Click to play a short excerpt of the song so you can make sure you want it.

HOT TIP: Look for the file you download in a folder called Downloads, which is contained in the My Documents folder.

5 Once the song has downloaded, double-click the file to play it using your default MP3 player.

6 Use a software program called a digital music player to listen to your digital music files. You can use what comes with your computer or install third-party programs.

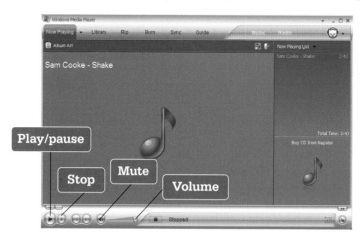

HOT TIP: You can also right-click a file and choose Play with Media Player to play it with Windows Media Player.

DID YOU KNOW?

If digital audio content is in the public domain, you can use it without paying for it. But you should pay a fee or get permission to listen to most content because it is protected by copyright. When you purchase music online, you obtain a digital licence that will allow you to play the audio file and may also place restrictions on whether you can copy the file to devices other than your computer.

WHAT DOES THIS MEAN?

MP3 (Motion Picture Experts Group Audio Level 3): A file format that compresses digital music so it is easily copied, removes extraneous sounds, and is ideal for downloading and storing on digital audio players.

WMA (Windows Media Audio): A Windows-based file format; files are about the same quality as MP3 but are compressed to only about half the size. This file format is often used for digital audio player storage.

AAC (Advanced Audio Coding): An audio file format used on a Mac and in the iTunes digital player.

Tune into internet radio

Yes, I listen to radio all day and all night. And I'm very particular about my programming. I like specific kinds of music, much of which is offbeat and can't be found on my local commercial (AM or FM) radio stations. A whole world of music, comedy and discussion awaits you when you tune into online radio. You can use Windows Media Player as your radio 'tuner', or find a website that has an internet radio stream and use a built-in player.

1 One way to find internet radio is to search for a topic on Google – for instance, 'Old Time Radio' – and go to a website that offers a radio stream.

2 Click on a link labelled Listen Live, Webcasts, Live Stream or something similar.

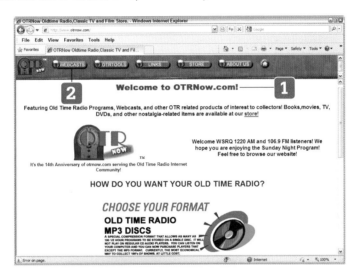

3 Many sites, like the one shown here, give you a choice of players. They provide their own – a player that pops up in a new browser window – or let you use your own software. Click the Listen with Our Player option for the pop-up window.

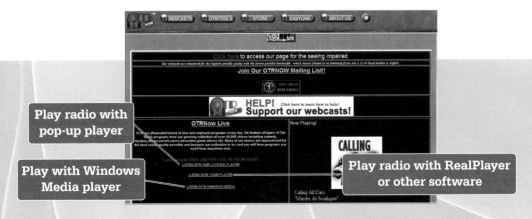

4 When the pop-up player opens, the audio will start playing automatically. Click Mute to silence the audio.

5 Click the Volume control to turn the sound up or down.

6 To use Windows Media Player as a radio 'tuner', click Start, click All Programs, click Accessories, and choose Windows Media Player to start up the application.

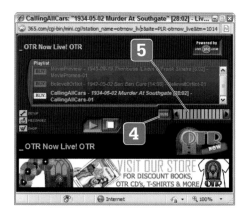

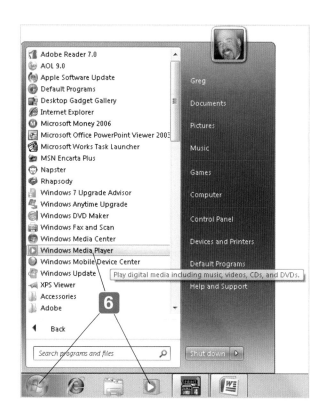

7 Click Guide.

8 Click internet Radio.

9 Choose the genre you want to listen to.

10 Click a radio station from the list displayed. The station starts playing.

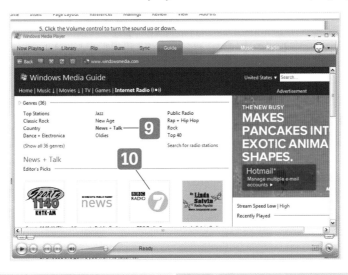

HOT TIP: In addition to the process described above, many over-the-air radio stations stream live broadcasts from their home pages. Look for the website of the radio station in your home town, or anywhere around the world. Many will have a Webcast or Listen Live link that lets you listen to them instantly.

Watch a YouTube video

If you ever want video entertainment that's absolutely free, turn to a site that's wildly popular around the globe: YouTube (the UK version is at http://www.youtube.com/?gl=GB&hl=en-GB). This site enables anyone to upload short video clips. As you might expect, the quality varies. But the range of content is virtually limitless, and you're likely to find old music videos, concert footage, and clips from virtually any kind of entertainment event.

1 Go to YouTube.

2 Click Browse to look for videos by category.

3 Type a word or phrase in the search box and click Search to look for video clips.

4 As you type in the search box, notice that YouTube suggests videos. Scroll down the list and click an option if it matches your criteria.

HOT TIP: You have to wait a few seconds for the video to load before you can move forwards or back through it.

5 Choose a video from the list of options.

6 At the top of the page, you'll see links to related videos that may be of interest.

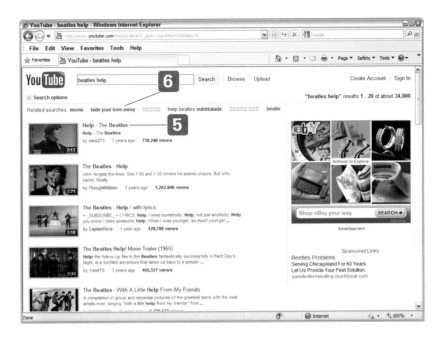

7 Adjust the volume to your preference.

8 Click to pause or play.

9 Move the slider to move ahead or back in the video.

Post your own YouTube video

From your grandson's dance recital to your spouse doing a belly flop into the pool, if you've got a video you can share it.

1 Click Sign In to sign into YouTube.

2 Click Upload.

3 Click here for technical tips on creating and uploading videos.

4 Click here to upload a video you have already taken and saved.

5 Click here to take a video right now if you have a camera connected to your computer, called a webcam.

ALERT: To post a video on YouTube, you need to be a registered user. It's free to register. You either create a free YouTube account or sign in with a Google account if you have one.

6 If you click the webcam option, click Allow.

7 Click Close.

8 Click Ready to Record. Your webcam will connect to YouTube. In a few seconds, you will begin recording.

9 Click here to adjust volume.

10 Click here to stop recording.

11 If you choose to upload a video and click the Upload a video link (see Step 4), click here to locate the file on your computer.

12 Select the file.

13 Click Open to upload the file.

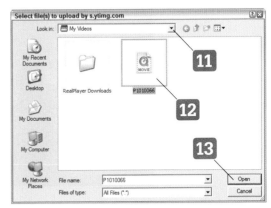

HOT TIP: Before you try to upload a video, make sure it meets the site's video requirements. The length must be no more than 10 minutes; 2–3 minutes is suggested. The video format needs to be H.264, MPEG-2 or MPEG-4. The resolution needs to be 640 × 360 or 480, and the maximum file size 1 GB.

ALERT: Be aware that when you post on YouTube, you have no way to restrict who sees it. Anyone in the world who finds your video through a search can play it. On Facebook, you can post videos and restrict them to those you designate as 'friends'.

Watch internet TV

If you're curious about the sort of televised entertainment you can watch with your computer and you haven't yet purchased a TV tuner add-on, you can watch a growing selection of internet TV using Media Center as your guide.

1 Under Movies + TV, click internet tv.

2 By default, top picks appears first. Click tv series to view available shows you can watch online.

3 Pass your mouse over the episode on the far right or left; when an arrow appears, click to scroll through different options.

4 Double-click a TV show to watch it.

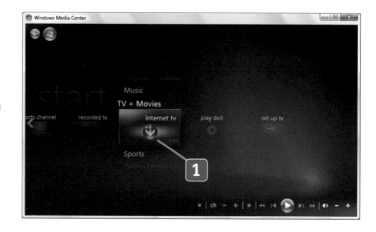

Watch live TV

I hate it when I miss my favourite TV shows. Now I'm good to go no matter what's on that night. Here's how to be a couch potato even if you're away from your couch. Media Center helps you watch TV, either on the internet or on live television.

1 Open Media Center.

2 If necessary, under TV + Movies, click set up tv.

3 Once you have set up your TV, move once to the right of recorded TV and click live Tv.

4 Position the mouse at the bottom of the live tv screen to show the controls you need.

HOT TIP: If you receive an error when you click live tv, either you don't have the television signal properly set up or you don't have a TV tuner. Many come with antennas, and you can find them for as little as £14.99 at Amazon.co.uk.

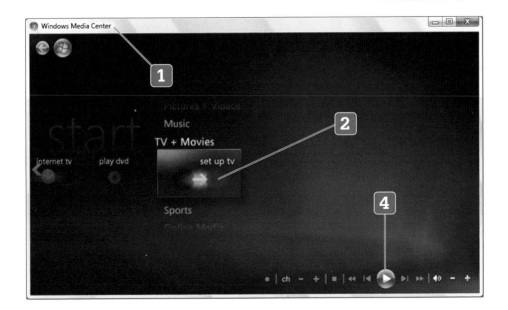

DID YOU KNOW?
There are lots of ways to navigate the Media Center. For instance, you can use the mouse, the arrow keys on the keyboard, or a remote control.

HOT TIP: If you don't have TV tuner hardware to hand, remember that many television networks archive recent episodes of their most popular programmes on their websites so you can view them any time, using programs such as Media Player.

Pause and rewind live TV

The hand that controls the remote control at home belongs to the person who rules the world. With Media Center on your computer, it's all at your fingertips as well.

1 Open Media Center.

2 Browse through TV shows and double-click one to play it.

3 Pass the mouse pointer over the bottom of the TV screen to display the controls.

4 Click the double vertical lines to pause the programme.

5 Click fast-forward or rewind to move back or forwards through the programme.

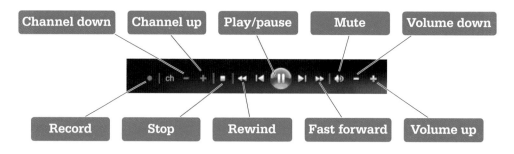

Channel down · Channel up · Play/pause · Mute · Volume down

Record · Stop · Rewind · Fast forward · Volume up

HOT TIP: Recorded TV is also an option with Media Player. If you record a TV show digitally and save it on a disk, you can use Media Center to play it.

HOT TIP: Pass your mouse over the contents of the Media Center window in order to see controls. When you pass your mouse pointer close to the right or left edge of the window, navigation arrows appear. When you pass your mouse over the bottom right corner of the window, the stop, play, back, forward, and other controls appear.

DID YOU KNOW?
You can fast-forward through the commercials by pressing pause at the beginning of the show: for a 30-minute show, pause for 10 minutes; for a 60-minute show, pause for 20 minutes.

Play a podcast

A podcast is an audio program that has been saved in digital format and posted on the internet so users with web browsers can download and play it. Because they are audio-only, they don't take up much disk space, which means you can download them to your computer and play them at your convenience, or stream them via your web browser. Podcasts come in countless varieties, ranging from the educational to inspirational to political.

1 Find a podcast on a website such as UK Podcasts (http://www.ukpodcasts.info).

2 Click on the link to the podcast.

3 Click one of the links for playing or saving the podcast. If you see a Play link, the default media player (most likely Windows Media Player) opens and begins to play the file.

4 Click here to save the file on your computer so you can play it.

? DID YOU KNOW?

Most podcasts are saved in a common web multimedia format such as MP3. Such files have the file extension .mp3 at the end of the filename. The application that will play the file is the one that is configured as the default player for MP3s. This may be Windows Media Player, but if you have installed another audio player on your computer, that application will launch instead. You can use Windows Media Player, if you prefer, by right-clicking the podcast filename and choosing Open with Windows Media Player.

8 Sending and receiving email

Introduction

Remember when you used to greet people with 'hello'? Now it seems the universal greeting is, 'Did you get my email?' While that's not always true, what is true is that email is a convenient option for keeping up with friends and family around the world. You save the cost of postage, you save the time and effort of writing and addressing a letter, and your message goes on its way in a matter of minutes. Rather than having to wait for the postman to arrive, email can show up in your inbox any time of the day or night. Once you're on the internet, an email account is available to you for no extra cost. This chapter introduces you to the basics of setting up your email account and sending and receiving messages.

Download Windows Live Mail

You have plenty of options for obtaining and sending and receiving email. If you get internet access from an ISP, that ISP will give you an email address. You can then use any email program to read mail and send your own messages. One option that is available to you no matter what operating system or internet provider you use is a Web-based email application called Windows Live. It's free to use – here is how to find and install it.

1 Start up IE8 and go to the Windows Live Essentials website: http://download.live.com.

2 Click Download to download a suite of Windows Live applications (you can read about them on this page). Choose programs to install including but not limited to: Windows Live Mail, Live Toolbar, Live Photo Gallery, and Live Messenger.

3 If you want to install only Windows Live Mail, click here.

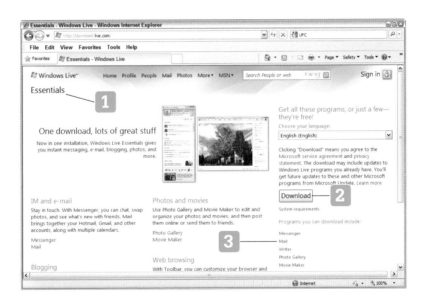

? DID YOU KNOW?

Email applications fall into two general categories: standalone email applications and Web-based email. Standalone applications are programs installed on your computer, such as Outlook or Thunderbird. You launch them from the Windows start menu. They take up memory on your computer, and your email messages are downloaded and stored on your file system. Web-based programs use a web browser interface. Messages are stored on the mail provider's server rather than on your computer.

4 After you click Download, click Run to actually download the set-up program – a program that sets up the application.

5 Click Run to install the application.

HOT TIP: Live ID lets you log into other Live services, sets up a webpage, and gives you an email account.

Sign up for Windows Live Mail

The first time you open Windows Mail, you're prompted to gather the information about your email address and mail servers. Getting and sending details, both personal and professional, is pretty much the point of email. So it stands to reason that you need to provide information to send and receive email.

1 Click Start, then click Windows Mail.

2 Click E-mail Account. Click Next.

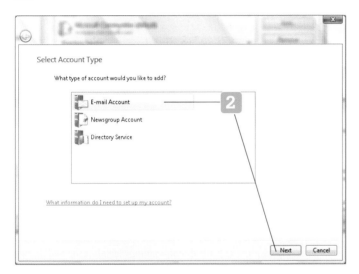

3 Type your display name. Click Next.

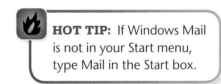

HOT TIP: If Windows Mail is not in your Start menu, type Mail in the Start box.

WHAT DOES THIS MEAN?

Display name: When you send an email message, this is the name that appears in the From line. Put your real name and address here rather than your email address.

User name: When you connect to your ISP's website to pay bills or change account information, you use a user name. The password is essential: it keeps your email and account information private. Usually passwords are case-sensitive.

Email address: When you obtained internet access from an internet service provider you received a default email address. If your user name is rkipling and your provider's URL ends with provider.co.uk, chances are your email address is rkipling@provider.co.uk. But check with your ISP to make sure.

4 Type your email address. Click Next.

5 Fill in the information for your incoming and outgoing mail servers. Click Next.

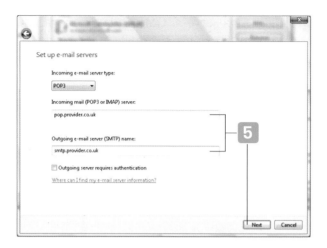

6 Type your email user name and password. Click Next.

7 Click Finish.

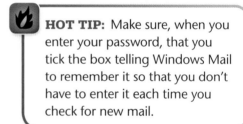

HOT TIP: Make sure, when you enter your password, that you tick the box telling Windows Mail to remember it so that you don't have to enter it each time you check for new mail.

DID YOU KNOW?

What you need to obtain from your internet service provider, if you haven't already, is an email address and the name of the servers that will route your outgoing and incoming mail.

HOT TIP: In case you don't want to use Windows Mail, or if you just want an alternative email service, you can get free email from Google (with its Gmail service) or Yahoo! (with Yahoo! Mail).

Configure Outlook email

If you have Microsoft Office installed, you have a built-in, full-featured email application called Microsoft Outlook at your disposal. The advantages of using your own application as opposed to a Web-based one are control and storage: you can generally store more email on your computer than on an account with an ISP. And you can organise email, block messages and perform advanced functions with Outlook that aren't available with a Web-based application. The following instructions are for Outlook 2010, and are similar for Office 2007.

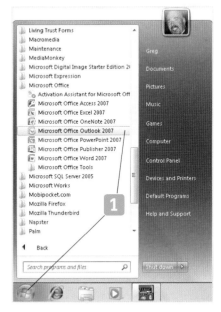

1 Click Start, click All Programs, click Microsoft Office, and click Microsoft Office Outlook 20xx (xx may stand for 07, 10, or another version).

2 When Outlook launches, click the File tab.

3 Click Account Settings, and choose Account Settings when it drops down.

4 Click New.

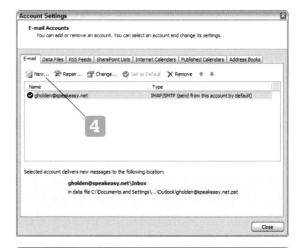

5 Enter your information in the Add New Account dialogue box.

6 Click Next.

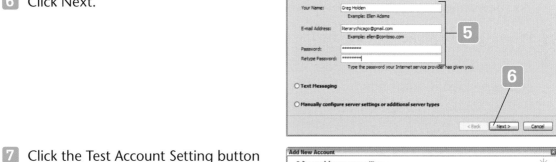

7 Click the Test Account Setting button to make sure that your mail works correctly and watch the status messages that appear.

8 After you have tested the settings, click Next and then Finish to add the account.

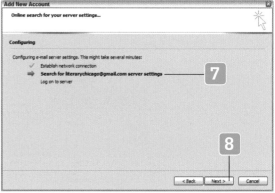

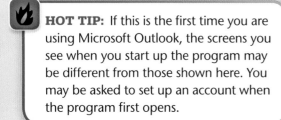

HOT TIP: If this is the first time you are using Microsoft Outlook, the screens you see when you start up the program may be different from those shown here. You may be asked to set up an account when the program first opens.

? DID YOU KNOW?
You can add as many email accounts as you want. Perhaps you can have one for family, one for personal, one for shopping, etc.

Compose and send a message

Much of the time, rather than responding to someone else's message, you'll be composing one from scratch. The process is almost the same as for responding to a message. But you need to make sure you have the correct email address for your recipient(s).

1 Click Create Mail.

2 In the To field, type the email address for the recipient.

3 Type a subject in the Subject field.

4 Type the message in the body pane.

5 Click Send.

HOT TIP: If you are sending your email to more than one recipient, separate each email address with a semicolon. The easy way to do this is to choose Tools and then click Select recipients to quickly add recipients from your Contacts list.

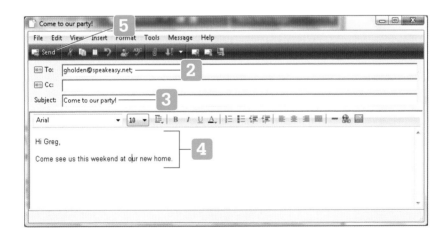

HOT TIP: Be precise when writing your subject line so your recipients can easily recall what the email was about.

? DID YOU KNOW?
If you want to let someone know what's in the email but don't expect them to respond, you can put them in the Cc line. If you don't want others to know that you sent the email to someone, you can put them in the Bcc line.

Read an email message

If you are wondering when your first email message will arrive, you don't have to wait long. Windows Mail provides you with your first welcome message. You can ask a friend or relative to send you another one just to test out the system.

1 Click the Send/Receive button.

2 Click the email once.

3 View the contents of the email.

4 Click the yellow bar if the email contains images that are not being displayed.

 HOT TIP: Clicking a new email message once rather than twice opens it in the current Mail application window. Double-clicking it opens it in a new window.

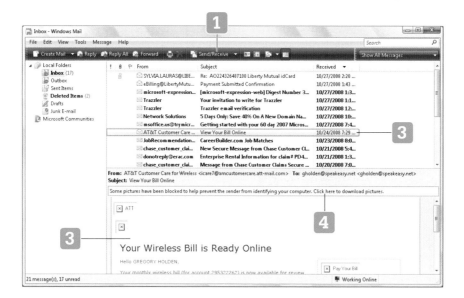

 ALERT: Email is received in the Inbox. If Inbox is not selected, do that first.

? DID YOU KNOW? You can adjust the size of the multiple panes that make up the Windows Mail window by clicking and dragging them.

Open and view an email attachment

When you see a paperclip, you know there's more than just the text in the body of the email. You may also have received a photo, document or video clip.

1 Click the email once in the Message pane.

2 Click the paperclip in the Preview pane.

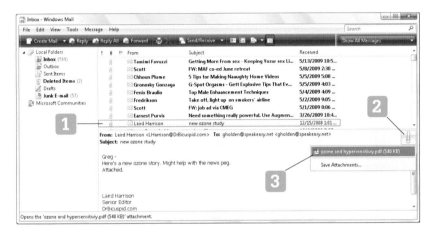

3 Click the name of the attachment.

4 Click Open.

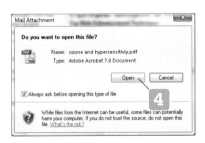

Reply to an email message

It's so great not to have to wait for ever knowing that you 'owe' someone a response. It's really quick and easy to reply to someone who has sent you an email.

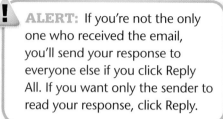

1 Select the email you want to reply to in the Message pane.

2 Click Reply.

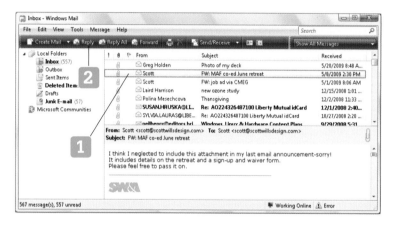

3 Make sure the email address is accurate.

4 Change the subject line in the Subject field if you wish.

5 Type the message in the body pane.

6 Click Send.

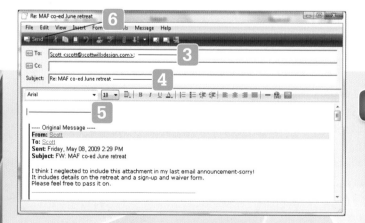

Attach an image to a message

If you know how to attach text, you know how to attach a photo or other image. You use Mail's Insert function to send the image along with your message, rather than cutting and pasting the image into the body of the message.

1 Click Create Mail.

2 Click Insert.

3 Click File Attachment.

4 If the item you want to attach is saved in your Documents folder, skip to step 6.

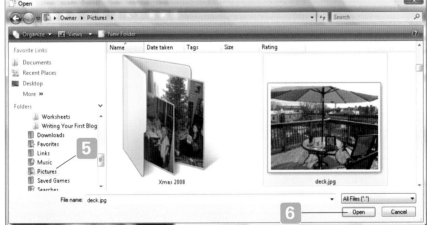

5 If the item you want to attach is not in the Documents folder, browse to the location of the folder.

6 Click the item that you want to add, and select Open.

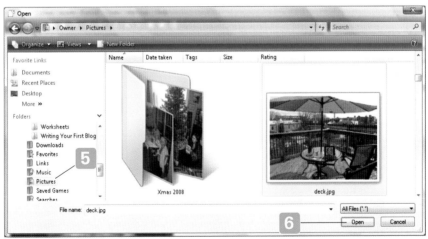

Add an email contact

It seems so long ago that you actually had to write down addresses in a little black book. Now, inside your personal folder, you can store your contacts in a Contacts folder. That way, you don't have to remember and then retype an email address each time you want to send someone a message.

1 From Windows Mail, click the Contacts icon on the toolbar.

2 Click File.

3 Pass your mouse over New and click Contact.

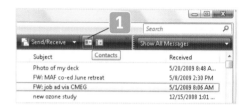

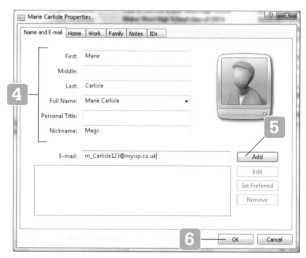

4 Type all of the information you want to add. Make sure you add information to each tab.

5 Click Add.

6 Click OK.

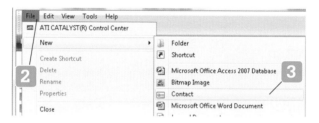

🔥 **HOT TIP:** There's a quicker way to add someone to your contacts. Right-click their name in your Inbox after you receive a message from them. Choose Add Sender to Contacts from the context menu. Their name and email address are added instantly.

❓ **DID YOU KNOW?**
Once you add someone to your Contacts list, you click the Contacts icon and then double-click their name in your list of contacts.

Send a message to multiple recipients

Form letters aren't always bad. Sometimes you need to make a general statement or announcement to a group of people. You can always individualise the response to give specific information to each person.

1 Click Create Mail.

2 In the To field, type the email addresses for each recipient, separated by a semicolon.

3 Type a subject in the Subject field.

4 Type the message in the body pane.

5 Click Send.

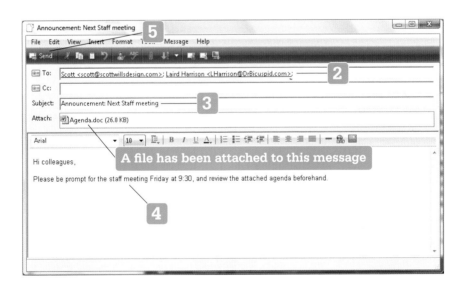

A file has been attached to this message

 HOT TIP: The easy way to send an email to multiple recipients is to choose Tools and then click Select recipients to quickly add recipients from your Contacts list.

 DID YOU KNOW?
If you receive an email message that was sent to you and others at the same time, you can reply to the entire group at once. Click Message and choose Reply to All, or press Ctrl+Shift+R.

Clean out your old email

There's a special satisfaction in having things neat and tidy. Plus, email sitting in either your Inbox or your Outbox takes up memory. Here's how to send an individual message to the trash and then empty the trash.

1 Right-click the email message.

2 Click Delete to send the message to Deleted Items.

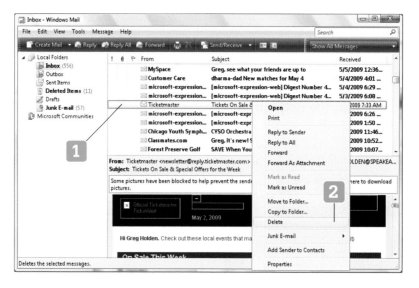

3 Right-click Deleted Items.

4 Click Empty 'Deleted Items' Folder.

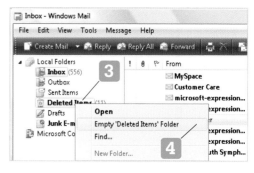

> ⚠ **ALERT:** Make sure you clean out your Sent Items folder. Every time you send a message, a copy sits in this folder until you clean it out.

🔥 **HOT TIP:** Select any email in any folder, and click the red X to delete it.

⚠ **ALERT:** Cleaning out your trash is especially important if your ISP sets a limit on the amount of storage space you can use for email. The more email sitting in your Inbox and other folders, the more memory you consume. If you go over your limit, you won't be able to send or receive email until you clean out old messages and free up more memory.

File away your email

The point of electronic files is that you don't have to clutter up your mind with things to remember. Putting email in folders is a good way to get organised.

1 Click the email message that you want to move in the Message pane.

2 Hold down the mouse while dragging the message to the new folder.

3 Repeat these steps for all the messages you want to move.

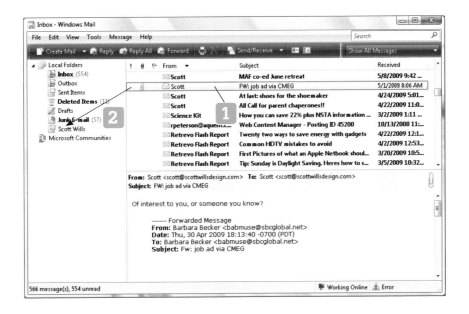

 HOT TIP: You can move multiple messages at the same time by selecting and moving them at once. To select a group of contiguous messages, click the first one in the group, press the Shift key, and click the last one in the group. To select a group of discontiguous messages, click the first one, press the Ctrl key, and click each one in turn.

 HOT TIP: You can also move a message by right-clicking it, choosing Move to Folder, and selecting the destination folder you want.

Create a signature file

You can add a 'deep thought' to appear at the bottom of each email message. Or you can stick to the basics and put your name and other particulars. It's great not to have to retype it every time.

1 Click Options and choose More options from the Windows Live Mail toolbar.

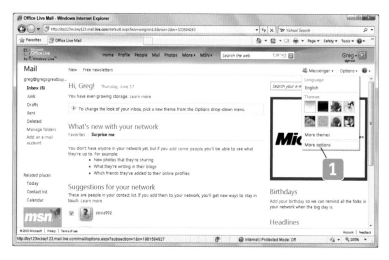

2 Click Personal e-mail signature under the heading Customise your mail.

3 Type your text and press Enter after each line.

4 Click Save.

ALERT: Make sure your comments are appropriate and that your information is something you want to share with each recipient.

Cut down on spam email

Spam is mail that is unwanted and that usually advertises products or services you aren't interested in. Some forms do bad things if you open them up, and some are just simply annoying. Here's how to make your email an area that spam can't enter.

1 Never give your email address to websites or companies or include your email in any registration you perform unless you are willing to accept junk email from the companies or their constituents.

2 If you are given the opportunity to opt out of receiving mailings from businesses from which you make purchases, do so.

3 Never buy anything advertised in a junk mail message or give money to anyone you don't know just on the basis of an email message.

> **! ALERT:** Don't assume that if it's in your Junk E-mail folder, it's junk. Check the contents every once in a while to make sure the folder didn't snag something that you want.

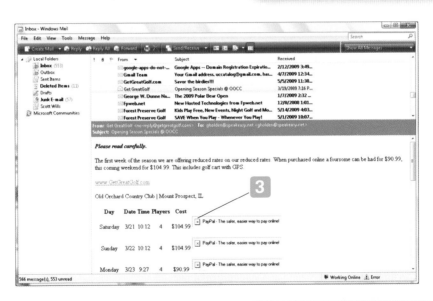

> **? DID YOU KNOW?**
> If it exists, it's a portal for hoaxes. Don't make a purchase from a junk email or send money for your portion of a winning lottery ticket or provide your credit card number to cure a 'sick' person.

> **? DID YOU KNOW?**
> If you give your email address to a company on its website or on a registration card, chances are you will be spammed by that company. It will also probably share this information, so you'll be spammed by others, too.

Forward an email message

If you want to share an email you've received, it's really easy. You don't even have to create more text unless you really want to add a personal touch.

1 Select the email you want to forward in the Windows Mail message pane.

2 Click Forward.

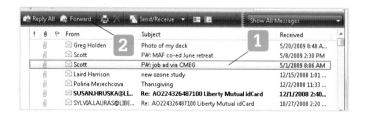

3 In the To field, type the email address for the recipient.

4 Type a subject in the Subject field if you wish, or leave the previous one in place.

5 Type the message in the body pane, above the text of the message you are forwarding.

6 Click Send.

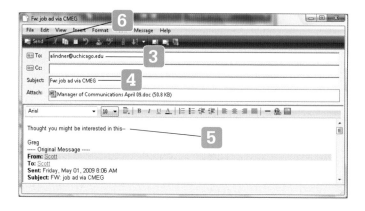

? DID YOU KNOW?
Your recipient will know the message has been forwarded because 'FW:' will be contained in the subject line by default.

! ALERT: Think before you send. If your recipient is really busy or doesn't have a lot of memory on their computer, they might not want to receive a forwarded message. Others can be offended by 'chain' emails, political statements or jokes.

9 Socialising on the Web

Introduction

It's great to keep in touch with long-time friends on the phone or by mail. It's also great to make new friends. Once you are on the internet and have become acquainted with email and web surfing, you can reach out to your family and friends in new ways. You'll also be able to answer the question your grandchildren are likely to ask: 'Where's your Facebook page?' Once you start networking on the internet, you'll be amazed at how easy it is to communicate with old school mates, long-lost family members, and both new and old acquaintances.

Create a Facebook page

Facebook is a social networking website – a site that includes tools for creating profiles, posting messages, and holding virtual conversations with your friends. On Facebook you can keep up with people you haven't seen in years … not to mention their children and grandchildren. Facebook has one big advantage over other venues that bring people together: you can pick and choose the people who see your personal information and who can communicate with you. You choose your Facebook 'friends' and decide how they can connect with you.

1 Launch IE8, and go to the UK Facebook page: http://en-gb.facebook.com.

2 Populate fields as you wish.

3 Click the green Sign Up button.

4 In the next screen, type the words shown and click Sign Up again.

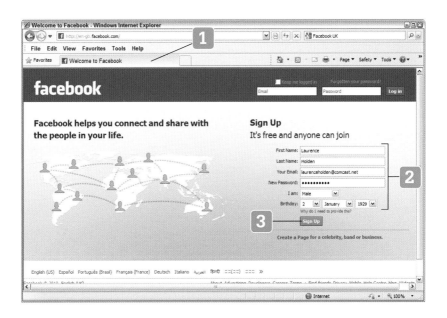

ALERT: Before you can use all of Facebook's features, you'll need to answer an email message that Facebook sends to you. Click on a link in the body of the message to verify your identity.

DID YOU KNOW?
Facebook's initial 'friend' suggestions come from your email address. It looks at your email contacts lists to see whether any users are already on Facebook.

5 In the next screen, Facebook suggests people you may know who are already on Facebook. If you see someone you know, click their name to add them as a 'friend'.

6 Click Continue.

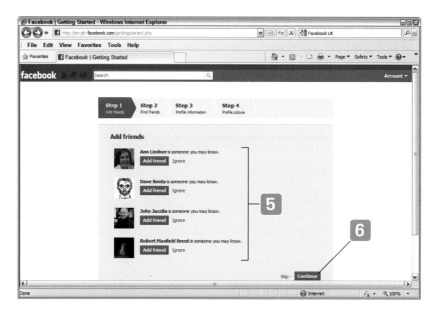

7 The next screen prompts you to find friends who are already on Facebook. Click Find Friends if you want to do this; click Skip this step to move on.

8 Fill out more information as appropriate to start building your Facebook profile.

9 Click Save & continue.

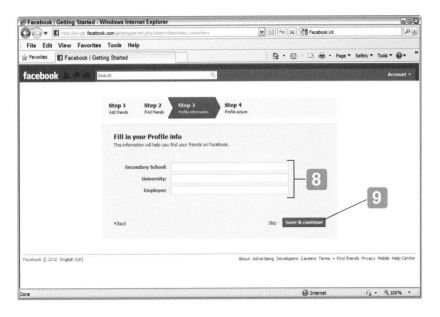

10 In the next screen, you are again encouraged to add friends you may know, based on the profile information you have entered. Click Skip or click Users and then click Save & continue.

11 Click Upload a photo, locate a photo on your computer, and click Open to upload it to Facebook.

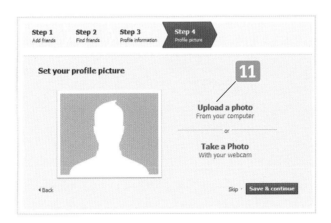

HOT TIP: You can search for friends at any time on Facebook – you don't have to do this when you first sign up.

HOT TIP: Be prepared before you start the process by having a digital photo of yourself that you like. Save the image in JPEG (Joint Photographic Experts Group) format.

Find a friend on Facebook

Facebook is different from other online venues in that it is based on friendships. You designate someone as a friend, then you can post messages which that person can see. When your friend posts a message, you can read it on your home page. You can search for friends at any time; the more friends you have, the more photos and news updates you'll have to read and respond to.

1 Click Friends in the links on the left side of your home page.

2 When the Friends page appears, review the suggestions Facebook gives you. Enter your email information and click Find friends to get Facebook to locate friends who are in your email address book or contacts list.

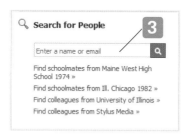

3 Further down on the Friends page, you can search for people by email or look for people who went to school with you and who are on Facebook.

ALERT: When you give Facebook your email address and password, you are giving sensitive information. If you don't trust Facebook with your email password, search for friends on your own.

Send a message on Facebook

How do you connect with people on Facebook? They may try to find you, for one thing: Facebook will send you notices of people who send 'friend requests', and you have the option of accepting or rejecting those requests. But you can also take the initiative and send someone a message.

1 Go to the individual's Facebook home page and click Send [person's name] a message.

2 Click here to 'poke' the person: this is Facebook's equivalent of tapping them on the shoulder and saying hello, without sending a message.

3 Type your message.

4 Attach an image, a video clip, or a link to a webpage.

5 When you're ready, click Send.

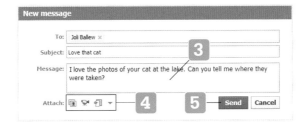

Post a comment on a Facebook page

Another way to communicate with your friends on Facebook is to post a comment. You can do this in one of two places: on your 'wall' (the place where you post notices and comments that everyone can see), or on someone else's 'wall'. You can either post a new comment, or add a remark or observation to a post someone else has made.

1 To post a comment on your own page, log onto Facebook. Or, if you are already logged on Facebook and are on someone else's page, click Home.

2 When your home page (otherwise known as your wall) appears, click the cursor in the message box at the top of the scrolling list of comments from you and all your friends. Then type your message.

3 Click one of these links to attach a video clip, image, or webpage link to your comment.

4 Click Attach.

5 Click Share to post your comment. It will appear on your wall and the wall of anyone who is your friend.

My friend Allan and I went to the Poetry Slam at the place where it originated, the Green Mill lounge on North Broadway. I forgot how much fun this is. One poet wrote about growing up in Des Plaines. I could sympathise.

🔗 Link ☒

Green Mill Cocktail Lounge
http://www.greenmilljazz.com/poetryslam....

In 1985 a construction worker and poet named Marc Smith (slampapi) started a poetry reading series at a Chicago jazz club, the Get Me High Lounge, looking for a way to breathe life into the open mike poetry format. ...

1 of 1 Choose a thumbnail
☐ No thumbnail

🔒 ▾ Share

? DID YOU KNOW?

The column in the centre of your home page is a scrolling wall. Comments posted by you and your friends appear there. The most recent comments appear at the top; earlier ones go underneath.

Comment on someone's posting on Facebook

Conversations on Facebook happen in a couple of ways. You can click on the Chat box in the bottom right-hand corner of a Facebook page and chat with someone who is online. Or you can comment on someone else's post – or someone's comment to someone's post. The resulting series of remarks forms a discussion.

1 To post a reply in response to someone else's posting, click once in the Write a comment link underneath it.

2 When a text box appears, type your comment.

3 Click Comment.

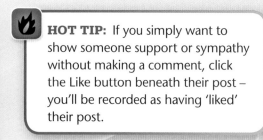

HOT TIP: If you simply want to show someone support or sympathy without making a comment, click the Like button beneath their post – you'll be recorded as having 'liked' their post.

Add photos to your Facebook profile

Facebook isn't just for posting words online, it's also fun to post photos. The photos you add can take one of two forms: you can add one or two individually as part of your profile, or you can group a set of photos in an album. Only those who are designated as your friends can see them, so you have a measure of privacy.

1 Go to your home page and click Profile.

2 Click the Photos tab.

3 Click Create a Photo Album.

4 Fill out the form naming and describing your album.

5 Choose who you want to have access to the album.

6 Click Create Album.

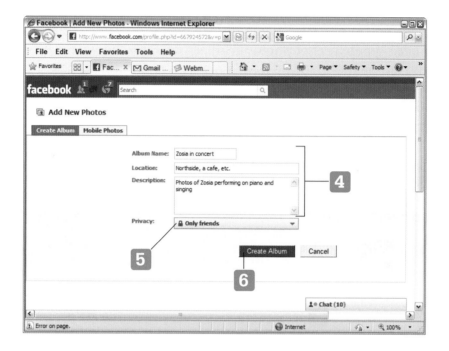

? DID YOU KNOW?

You can change your privacy settings so that everyone can see your photos, or only designated individuals. Click Account in the upper right-hand corner of any Facebook page and click Privacy Settings to adjust who can see different parts of your profile.

! ALERT: It's a good idea to review your privacy settings even if you don't plan to change them – you may not agree with the default settings Facebook gives you.

Make a phone call with your computer

Voice over internet Protocol (VoIP) is a technology that you can use to make calls to anywhere in the world from your computer. All you need is a microphone designed to work with a computer, an internet connection, and software such as Skype that's designed to permit such communications. What's more, a webcam can add video to create a video phone system.

1 Go to Skype's UK home page (http://www.skype.com/intl/en-gb).

2 Click Download. Follow the steps on subsequent screens to download and install Skype.

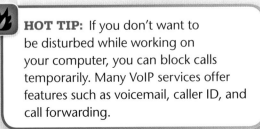

HOT TIP: If you don't want to be disturbed while working on your computer, you can block calls temporarily. Many VoIP services offer features such as voicemail, caller ID, and call forwarding.

3 Choose a Skype screen name.

4 Upload a small photo you have saved in JPEG format.

5 Search for contacts you might know and click one.

6 Click Call to initiate your Skype call.

Carry on a video conversation

Once you have Skype installed, you can carry on either audio or video conversations, depending on the hardware you have to use with your computer. If you and your friend have a webcam (a small camera that plugs into your computer and lets you take video while you're sitting at it), you can carry on a video conversation.

1 Purchase a webcam. You can find one at any computer store or at many large general merchandise stores such as Tesco.

2 Install the software included with the camera on a CD.

3 Plug the camera into one of your computer's USB ports.

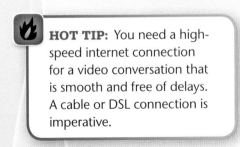

HOT TIP: You need a high-speed internet connection for a video conversation that is smooth and free of delays. A cable or DSL connection is imperative.

4 Start up Skype and click one of your contacts' names.

5 Click the Video call button, which appears only if you have a webcam connected.

6 Move the slider to the left or right to adjust the volume.

7 When you've finished, click End call.

Send a text message with Skype

What happens if you make a call and someone isn't at their computer? The call won't go through. But you can still leave a text message for that person and when they launch Skype, your message will be visible. You can also type text messages while you are communicating with someone, in case your connection is poor or malfunctioning.

1 Click the name of the person you want to contact.

2 Click once in the text box at the bottom of the Skype window.

3 Type your message.

4 Press Enter to send your message to the other person.

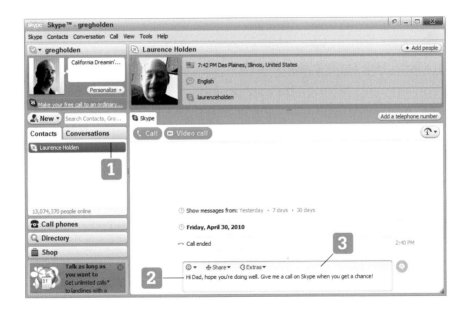

 HOT TIP: If one of your contacts is at their computer and Skype is active (if the program has been launched and running), you'll see a green icon next to their name. If the user's computer is on but Skype is not active, you'll see a yellow icon next to the person's name. You can call the person, but they may not be close enough to answer. If they are away, you'll see a white icon next to their name.

Create a blog

The term 'blog' comes from the phrase 'web log'. It's a very effective way of inviting others to share their ideas on your thoughts.

1 Create a blog space. You can usually use your email or you can go to a blog space service such as Google's free Blogger (www.blogger.com). In any case, it's often free and simple to sign up.

2 Choose your settings after deciding whether to allow public access or to allow only those you know to participate.

3 Decide whether you want a photo of yourself on your blog and determine other blog design elements. In addition to choosing colours and fonts, you can decide the design of postings, archives of older postings and responses.

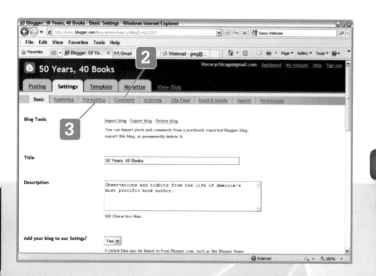

HOT TIP: If you decide you're going to start a blog, you have to attend to it frequently to keep it in shape. Try to make updates every day or two. If you'll be otherwise occupied for a while, tell people your site will be temporarily quiet.

HOT TIP: Allowing others to come to your blog is fun, but it's also interesting to read and respond to comments from others. Ask your friends and family members if they have blogs and find others that are open to the public.

Comment on someone else's blog

A blog may seem like a one-way means of communication, but it's not. One of the good features about blogs is that you, or others, have the opportunity to post comments in response to posts. The resulting dialogues can give your blog life and keep visitors coming back.

1 Access the post that interests you.

2 Click the Comments link and review the most recent comments from others.

3 Sign in if required.

4 Type your comment.

5 Click Publish Your Comment.

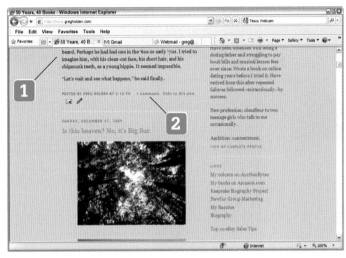

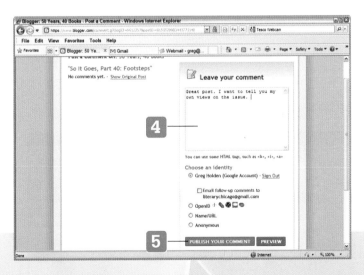

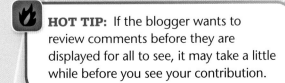

HOT TIP: If the blogger wants to review comments before they are displayed for all to see, it may take a little while before you see your contribution.

Subscribe to a blog feed

We're always looking for shortcuts, and here's a way to stay up to date with what's happening with blogs of interest to you without spending your life on the computer.

1 Access the blog that provides the feed.

2 Make sure you have the feed you want, then click the icon.

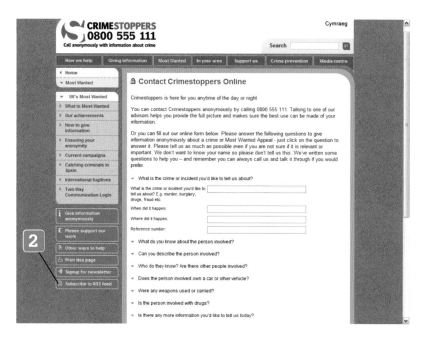

3 Click the link that lets you subscribe to this feed.

4 When the dialogue box appears, click Subscribe.

5 To access your feed, click the Favorites button in IE8 and click the Feeds tab.

6 Double-click the name of the feed you want to read.

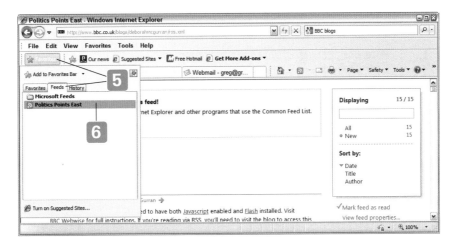

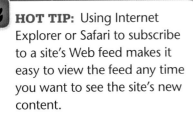 **HOT TIP:** Using Internet Explorer or Safari to subscribe to a site's Web feed makes it easy to view the feed any time you want to see the site's new content.

 **DID YOU KNOW?** If you hear about an RSS feed, it stands for Really Simple Syndication.

Get started with Twitter

With Twitter, you have fewer than 140 characters to answer the basic question: What are you doing? Besides these messages, which are called 'tweets', you can also point out a new item on a website or contact another Twitter user.

1 Start up IE8 and go to the Twitter site, www.twitter.com.

2 Click the Join Today link.

3 Type the user name you want in the Username text box.

4 Type the password of your choice.

5 Type your email address.

6 Read the terms of service.

7 Click Create my account.

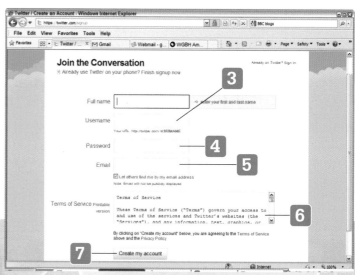

? DID YOU KNOW?

Microblogging is a term used for Twitter posts. It is a form of blogging where each post is a very short message.

10 Buying and selling online

Introduction

Once you have learned to establish a presence on the Web, you can use that presence to make some money. If you need to clear out your storage space, you can put a few items for sale on Craigslist. If you want to sell on a regular basis, you can create an eBay Store. You can sell books or CDs on Amazon.com's marketplace, or put your original artwork on products you sell via CafePress. This chapter introduces you to some of the many ways to sell items online.

Shop on Craigslist

Have you looked through the For Sale or other classified ads in your local newspaper recently? You've probably noticed that they are dwindling in size. That's happening because of competition from sites like Craigslist. Craigslist is an online classified ad website. Instead of the tiny ad space available in a newspaper, Craigslist gives sellers a whole webpage on which to sell a single item, complete with a detailed description and photos. Ads are updated continually on a 24/7 basis.

1 Launch IE8, and go to the main Craigslist UK website (http://london.craigslist.co.uk).

2 Scan the list of local Craigslist sites in the UK for a city near yours, if necessary, and click the one closest to you.

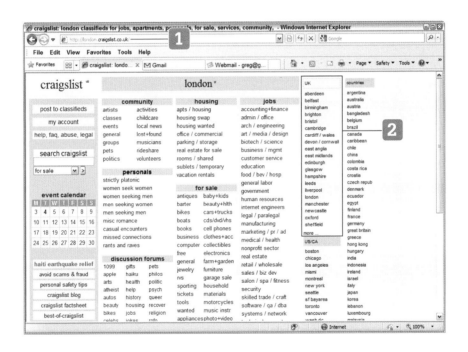

HOT TIP: Craigslist is not the only online classified website to cover the UK. Also try Classifieds.co.uk (http://www.classifieds.co.uk), for instance.

3 Like many websites, Craigslist lets you shop by searching or browsing through categories and subcategories. To search, select a category from this drop-down list.

4 Enter a keyword and press the search craigslist button.

5 You can also click through categories and subcategories if you prefer.

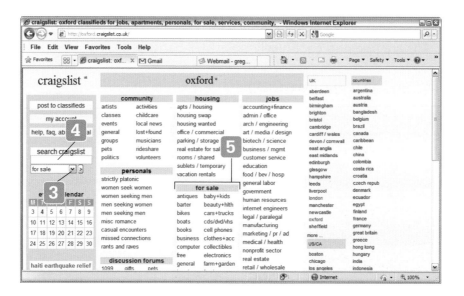

6 Scroll through items by date.

7 Make a note of items that are not in your local area.

8 When you see an item that interests you, click the link to it.

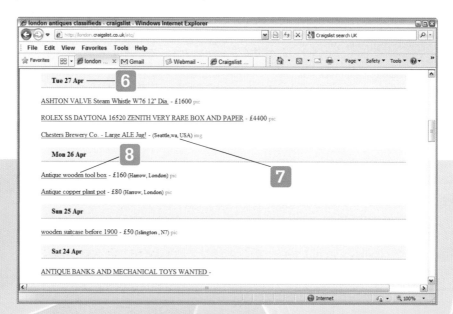

9 Read the description and view the photos.

10 Click here to email the seller to express interest or to ask for more information.

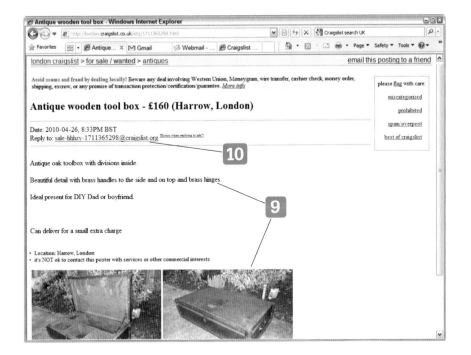

HOT TIP: On Craigslist, you can view items for sale in only one local area at a time. If you don't see something you want in your own area, check nearby towns. Or try a search service that covers all of the UK such as the one at http://www.seekyouritem.com/cl.

ALERT: The vast majority of transactions on Craigslist are legitimate. But you can't really judge who is posting on the site. Be sceptical, ask questions, and take care before you commit money – make sure the sale is not a scam.

Place an ad on Craigslist

One reason Craigslist is so popular is that it's free to individuals who have something to put up for sale. Another reason is that it's easy to sell. You don't have to take photos of an item you have for sale, but your ad will get more attention if you do. First, take 1–5 images of your item and save them in JPEG format. Write a sales description that includes details such as the size, date, model number, and so on. Then follow these steps.

1 Navigate to the category on Craigslist that covers your item, or where others are offering similar items for sale.

2 Click the [post] link at the top of the category page.

3 Read the advice about avoiding scams on Craigslist.

4 Click the subcategory that matches your item.

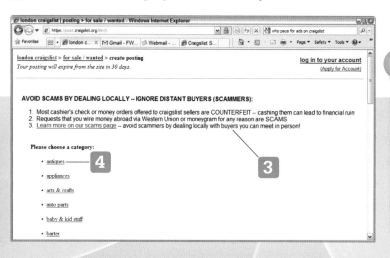

? DID YOU KNOW?

Businesses offering property for sale or rental in some cities, companies with job listings, and people who want to offer therapy and 'adult services' are charged a fee for listing on Craigslist.

5 Type a title and location and your email address.

6 Type your description.

7 Click Add/Edit Images.

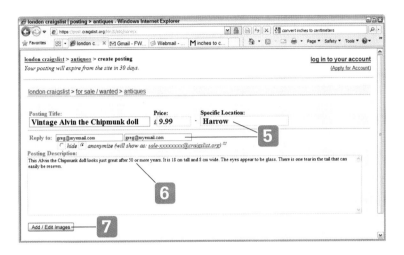

8 In the bottom half of the same page, a new section opens with four buttons labelled Browse. Each button lets you upload an image from your computer. Click Browse, locate the image, and double-click it to upload it.

9 Repeat step 8 up to three times for four images of your item.

10 Click Continue

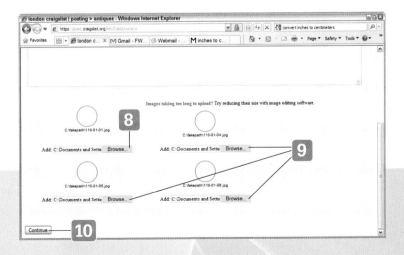

11 Review your listing before it goes online.

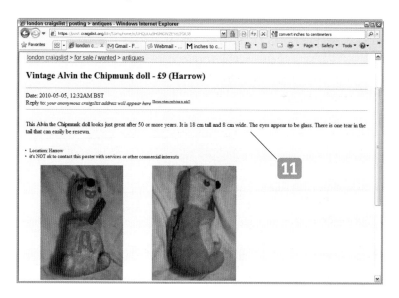

12 Click Continue.

13 On the next page, click Accept the Terms of Use.

14 Click a verification code and your email address.

15 Craigslist sends you an email. Click the link in the email, which takes you back to Craigslist. Click Publish to post your sale online.

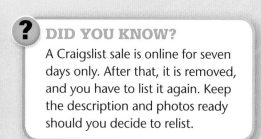

DID YOU KNOW?
A Craigslist sale is online for seven days only. After that, it is removed, and you have to list it again. Keep the description and photos ready should you decide to relist.

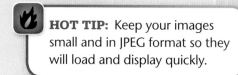

HOT TIP: Keep your images small and in JPEG format so they will load and display quickly.

Set up an eBay store

Who would have guessed that you'd end up as a shopkeeper? eBay gives everyone the chance to set up a virtual storefront for a modest monthly fee. Still, even if your items sell only once in a while, it's a good option to get rid of some of that clutter and pad your pockets in the process.

1 Go to eBay's UK site (http://www.ebay.co.uk).

2 Click Sign in, and sign in with your eBay username and password. If you aren't yet an eBay registered user, click the Register button and follow the steps on subsequent pages.

3 Go to the eBay Shops hub page (http://stores.shop.ebay.co.uk/_stores/hub).

4 Click Open a Shop.

? DID YOU KNOW?

A Basic Shop costs £13.03 per month, a Featured Shop costs £43.47 per month, and an Anchor Shop costs £304.34 per month.

5 Click the button next to Basic Shop.

6 Type a name for your shop.

7 Click Continue.

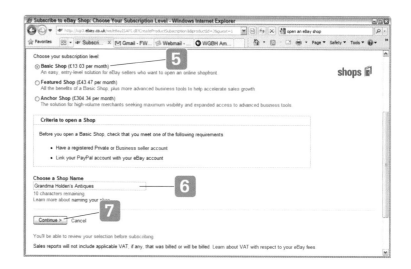

8 On the next two pages, select features, review terms and the monthly fee, and click Subscribe.

9 Once you have opened your shop, you can create sales categories for it, and add items for sale.

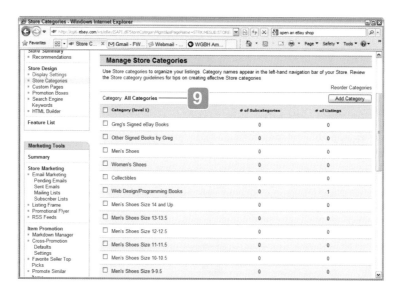

Set up an account with PayPal

It's hard to imagine life without credit cards. But there are often those pesky fees, and it's wise to discriminate about who you give information to. PayPal is like an escrow service that debits buyers' accounts and credits the accounts of sellers.

1 Launch IE8, and go to the PayPal UK page (http://www.paypal.co.uk).

2 Click the Sign Up button.

3 Click the Get Started button in the Premier account section.

4 Follow the instructions to fill out registration forms.

5 Click Agree and Create Account.

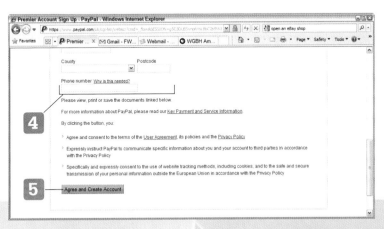

? DID YOU KNOW?

PayPal enables you to be paid online for items you sell on eBay. But it's not free – PayPal takes a fee each time money is transferred to your account.

Sell on Amazon.com

When you hear Amazon.com, you probably think 'books'. But many other items, from household goods to electronics, are also sold on the site. You can add to the marketplace by putting your own items for sale. If you see something being sold on the site, and you have the same item, you can put it up for sale as well.

1 Go to Amazon.com's UK site (http://www.amazon.co.uk) and navigate to the Books section.

2 Search for a book you have and want to sell.

3 When the product page for the book appears, click the Sell yours here link.

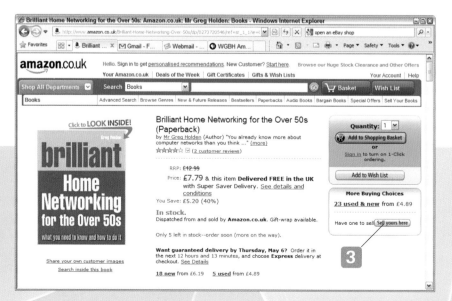

4 Choose the term that describes the condition of your copy of the book.

5 Type a few descriptive words about your book.

6 Click Continue.

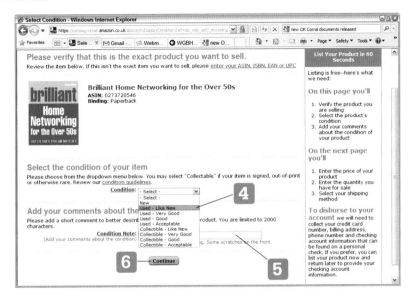

7 Type the price for your item.

8 Change the quantity, if necessary.

9 Change shipping information, if necessary.

10 Click Continue.

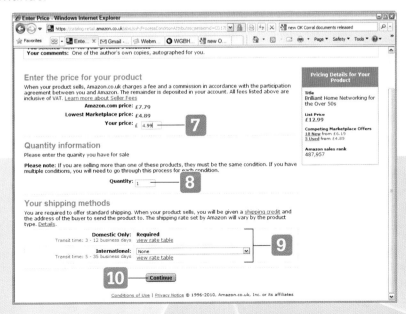

11 Enter your Amazon.com email address and password.

12 Read the sellers' terms, and click Continue.

13 Choose a credit card from the list.

14 Click Continue.

15 Enter your nickname and a daytime phone number to verify your identity.

16 Click Call Me Now. Answer the phone, type the PIN number supplied, and hang up. Then click Continue.

17 Review your item information and then click Confirm to list your item for sale.

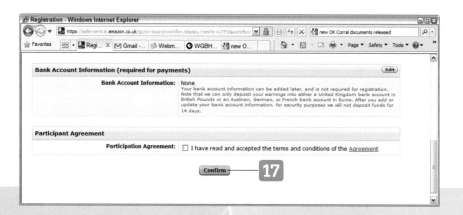

? DID YOU KNOW?

If your item doesn't sell within 60 days, Amazon.com closes your listing at no charge to you. Or you can relist the item if you so desire.

Sell on CafePress

Maybe you now have the time to get seriously into arts and crafts. But what do you do when you've given all your samples away? This site allows you to use your own artwork. They do the heavy lifting of printing it on t-shirts, mouse pads, mugs, cards, aprons, and other household items. The merchandise is really attractive and high quality. And you can set your own price.

1 Go to the CafePress website (www.cafepress.com/cp/info/sell).

2 Click the Start Selling Now! button.

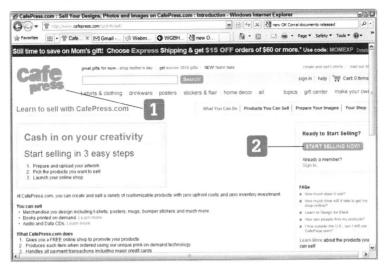

3 Assign yourself a username and password.

4 Click Join Now.

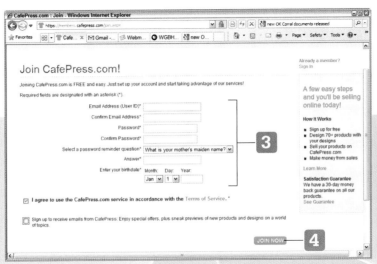

5 Fill out a survey, choose a name for your store and click Open a Basic Shop to set up your store.

6 Click Products under the Shop Management heading.

7 Click Add a Product.

8 Tick boxes next to the types of items you want to sell.

9 Click [select image] to add an image that you drew or photographed earlier, and that you can have printed on the merchandise you have selected. Click Add These Products to select specific items you want to sell, then click Preview This Page to review your shop to make sure it looks the way you want.

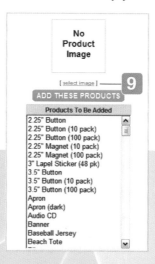

Top 10 Internet Problems Solved

Introduction

Many of the problems with using the internet involve getting or maintaining a connection. Luckily for you, this is a common situation and a well-known set of steps is available to get you out of trouble. Windows 7 also contains some settings that make your computer easier to use and that help solve email problems.

Problem 1: I've lost my internet connection. How do I reconnect?

Sooner or later, you'll probably encounter problems connecting to the internet. Before you call your internet service provider's support staff, there are some tried-and-tested approaches you should take.

1. Make sure your modem, router, cables, and other hardware are properly connected, plugged in and turned on.

2. If your computer uses a wireless connection to get online, restart your computer.

3. Open the Network and Sharing Center.

4. Click the red X.

5. Perform the steps presented in the Windows Network Diagnostics dialogue box.

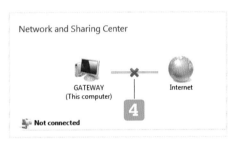

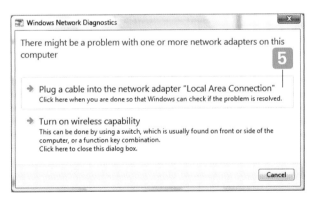

ALERT: When restarting a cable or satellite modem, you need to turn it off completely first. That involves removing any batteries.

? DID YOU KNOW?
You need to turn off all hardware, including the computer, if you're prompted to reset your broadband or satellite connection. Restarting should be done in the following order: cable/satellite/DSL modem, router, laptops.

Problem 2: Can Windows diagnose and repair my network connection?

If you are having trouble getting on the internet, the first step is to use the built-in Diagnose and Repair tool that comes with Windows 7. If this first option doesn't work, you can try other problem-solving options such as Network Diagnostics.

1 Right-click the network connection icon in the system tray and choose Troubleshoot problems.

2 The Windows Network Diagnostics utility runs automatically. When it presents you with an option, click it. Follow the steps shown in subsequent screens to repair the connection.

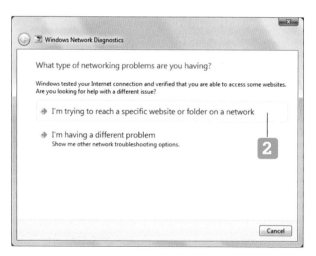

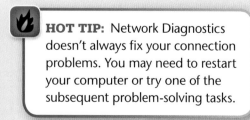

HOT TIP: Network Diagnostics doesn't always fix your connection problems. You may need to restart your computer or try one of the subsequent problem-solving tasks.

Problem 3: My modem and router are disconnected. How do I reset them?

The most fundamental problem with a network is one you have probably encountered from time to time: you can't connect to a central server, to the internet, or to other networked devices. The best strategy is to be systematic about the problem. If the problem is with your internet connection, start at the point where the internet connection comes into your house, and work from there. Sooner or later, you'll identify the problem.

1 Check your broadband modem: verify that the DSL or cable modem light is on and not blinking.

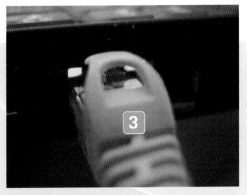

2 Check out the router and make sure the internet light is on. If it is, check the cables are plugged into the router's ports and make sure they are firmly connected. A light should be lit on the front of the router for each computer on your network. If the internet light is out, reset the router by turning it off and then back on.

3 If the router connections are functioning correctly, move to your computer. If you use Ethernet, make sure the cable is plugged securely into your computer's Ethernet port.

4 If the cable is plugged in but it's still not working, restart the computer.

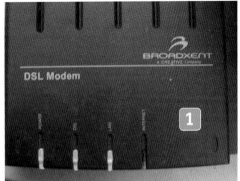

5 After the restart, if the connection is still broken, replace the cable to make sure it's not broken.

6 If you have a wireless rather than a wired connection, right-click the network connection icon in the system tray and choose Troubleshoot problems.

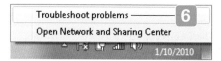

7 The Windows Network Diagnostics utility runs automatically. When it presents you with an option, click it. Follow the steps shown in subsequent screens to repair the connection.

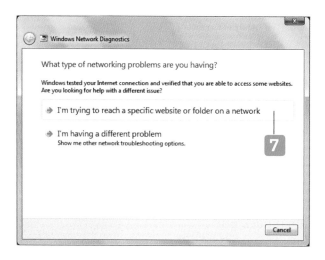

Problem 4: I have to reset my network connection. How do I do this?

If you are having trouble getting online and your modem and router are functioning properly, you'll need to reset your internet connection. One option is to 'release and renew' the connection using a command-line interface.

1 Click Start, type **cmd** in the Start box, and press Enter.

2 At the command prompt, type **ipconfig /release**, then press Enter.

3 When you see the IP address listed as 0.0.0.0, type **ipconfig /renew** at the command prompt.

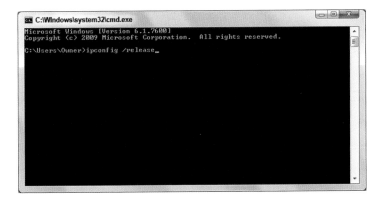

Problem 5: My computer says it cannot acquire a network address. What can I do?

To connect to the internet or another network, your computer needs to have a special identifier called an IP address. In most cases, you don't need to worry about choosing this special ID number – Windows will use the Dynamic Host Configuration Protocol (DHCP) system software utility to connect to cause one to be assigned to you automatically. This utility connects to a DHCP server, either in your router or provided by your internet service provider. The server dynamically assigns network addresses to computers on a network. In case you have trouble getting online, it's a good idea to verify that DHCP is enabled.

1 Click Start.

2 In the field that appears above the Start button, type Network and then click the Network and Sharing Center link (in the Control Panel group) when it appears near the top of the Start menu.

3 In the View your basic network information and set up connections window that opens, click the name of the current network connection, which appears as an underlined link.

4 In the Status window that opens, click the Properties button.

5 On the Properties sheet, click internet Protocol Version 4 (TCP/IPv4) and then click Properties.

6 In the internet Protocol Version 4 (TCP/IPv4) window that appears, make sure that the Obtain an IP address automatically and the Obtain DNS server address automatically radio buttons are both selected. This means that the DHCP server will automatically assign an IP address for you.

7 Click OK to close this window and then click OK to close the Properties sheet for your connection.

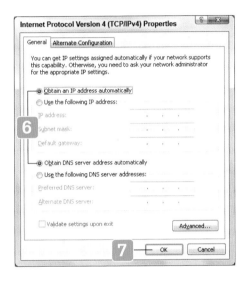

HOT TIP: You can also click the Network Connection item and choose Open Network and Sharing Center as described earlier in this chapter. This path is just an alternative method for opening the Network and Sharing Center.

Problem 6: I have vision problems. How can I make internet content easier to use?

If you have vision problems, you can make webpages and other internet content easier to see. If you are blind, you or a friend can optimise your computer so that it can be used without a display.

1 Open the Control Panel.

2 Click Ease of Access.

3 Click Ease of Access Center.

4 Click Make the computer easier to see.

5 Click one of the High Contrast options.

6 To get your computer to read text and descriptions to you, tick Turn on Narrator or Turn on Audio Description.

7 Click Save.

8 To make objects on your monitor appear larger without having to change screen resolution, click Change the size of text and icons.

9 To activate an interactive magnifying glass on screen, click Turn on Magnifier.

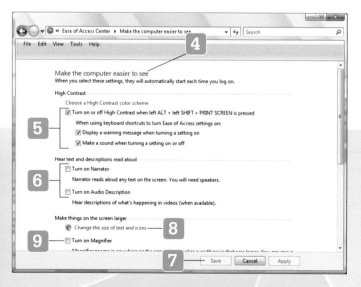

! ALERT: You need to have external speakers or headphones connected to your computer if you plan to use the Narrator or Audio Description features.

? DID YOU KNOW?
When you choose one of the vision enhancements, they will start automatically each time you log onto Windows. You will have to deselect them from the Make the computer easier to see screen if you want to disable them.

10 If you clicked Change the size of text and icons, click Larger scale to make text bigger.

11 Click OK.

12 If you clicked Turn on Magnifier, the Magnifier appears immediately at the top of your screen. Move the mouse arrow around the screen, and the contents appear above.

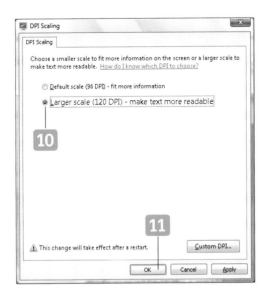

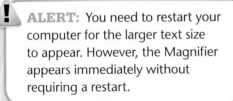

ALERT: To turn off the Magnifier, you have to untick the Turn on Magnifier box.

ALERT: You need to restart your computer for the larger text size to appear. However, the Magnifier appears immediately without requiring a restart.

HOT TIP: Click Custom DPI to enter a number larger than 120 DPI (dots per inch) if you need text to be even bigger than 'larger scale'.

Problem 7: I find my computer screen hard to read. What can I do?

If you are used to reading only on paper, suddenly trying to read text and view lists of files and folders on a computer screen can be disorienting. Not to worry: you have several options available to you for making your computer's contents more readable.

1 Turn up the brightness on your monitor: open the Mobility Center and move the brightness slider to the right.

2 Change the resolution: open the Control Panel.

3 Under Display, click Adjust screen resolution.

4 Move the slider to the left to make the resolution smaller, which makes the content appear bigger.

5 Click OK.

Appearance and Personalization
Change desktop background
Customize colors
Adjust screen resolution

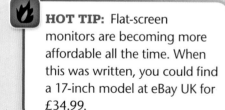
HOT TIP: Flat-screen monitors are becoming more affordable all the time. When this was written, you could find a 17-inch model at eBay UK for £34.99.

ALERT: Changing screen resolution is an option, but if you make icons on your screen too big, you might lose sight of some of them. Before you try the smallest resolution (800 × 600), try an in-between resolution such as 1024 × 768.

Problem 8: Outlook won't send or receive email. What can I do?

It's not unusual to press Outlook's Send and Receive button only to discover that the program cannot perform this function. Usually, it means Outlook is unable to connect to your email server. Before you call your internet service provider's support staff, you should try a few debugging procedures on your own. Often, you can troubleshoot the problem yourself.

1 If you are connected to the internet via an Ethernet cable, make sure the cable is plugged in securely both to your computer and to your router.

2 Point to the network icon in the system tray. If you are attempting to retrieve email from a remote server rather than your company or organisation's network, you should see the message Access: Local and internet. If you see the Message Access: Local Only, you are not connected to the internet.

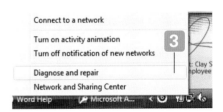

Network icon

3 If you are not connected to any network or you see the Local Only message, right-click the Network icon and choose Diagnose and repair.

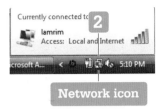

4 Wait for the network diagnostics tool to investigate the problem. Follow the recommendations in the diagnostics report.

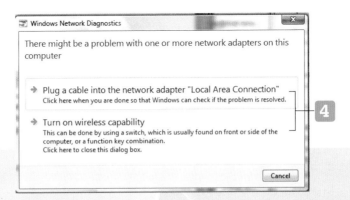

5 If you have a wireless connection, right-click the network icon and choose Connect to a network.

6 Choose your preferred network from the list and click Connect.

7 If you cannot connect, or if you connect but still don't have internet access, restart your computer.

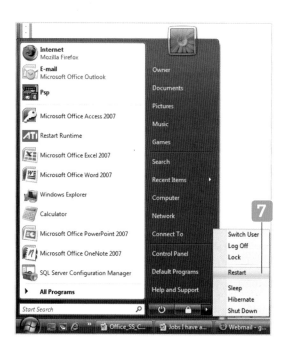

Problem 9: I'm getting too much on junk email (spam). How do I stop it?

Some spam is annoying and some is downright offensive. Here's how to get less of what you don't want by enabling the junk email filter in Windows Mail.

1 If Windows Mail detects an email message that is potentially harmful and it displays this dialogue box, click Junk E-mail Options.

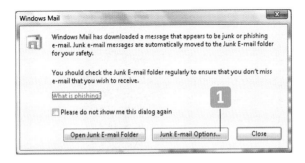

2 If you want to manually adjust junk mail settings, click Tools.

3 Click Junk E-mail Options.

4 From the Options tab, make a selection.

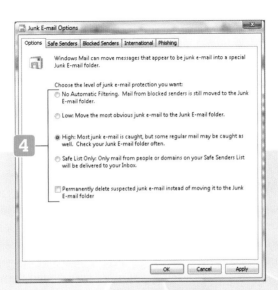

5　Click the Phishing tab.

6　Select Protect my Inbox from messages with potential Phishing links.

7　Select Move phishing E-mail to the Junk Mail folder.

8　Click OK.

Problem 10: I need to remove programs I don't want

Conventional wisdom dictates that if an article of clothing has hung in your wardrobe for more than a year without being worn, it should be given away. The same principle applies to your computer. You pick up a number of applications in the course of your web surfing. If you haven't used one of those applications for a long time, you can safely remove it to save disk space.

1 Click Start, then click Control Panel.

2 In Control Panel, click Uninstall a program.

3 Scroll through the list. Click a program name if you want to uninstall it.

Programs
Uninstall a program
Change startup programs

4 Click Uninstall.

5 Follow the prompts to uninstall the program.

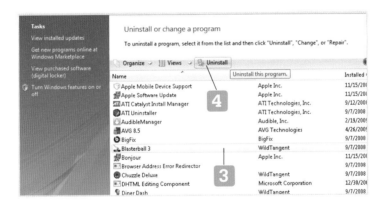

? DID YOU KNOW?

Your computer may have come with programs that you don't need. Manufacturers also add applications that you don't want, such as office suites or games. If you don't use it, lose it.